Aaron's Mailbox

Aaron's Mailbox

Gayle Guadagnolo

Mill City Press

FOREWARD BY INTUITIVE MEDIUM, MELANIE MAY

MILL CITY PRESS, INC.

212 3RD AVENUE NORTH, SUITE 290

MINNEAPOLIS, MN 55401

612.455.2294

WWW.MILLCITYPUBLISHING.COM

ISBN-13: 978-1-937600-21-1

LCCN: 2011939548

COVER DESIGN AND TYPESET BY TIM PARLIN

PRINTED IN THE UNITED STATES OF AMERICA

TABLE OF CONTENTS

PART I

My Wish For You

We live our lives, taking each day as it comes, content and happy. Then suddenly, for some of us, life, as we knew it, changes in an instant.

The things that we thought were normal are no more. The unimaginable things that we would never dare think about now consume our every thought. The little bit of control that we thought that we had is completely ripped from our grasp, and we are left with this new, unfamiliar existence, wondering what the hell just happened and not knowing what to do.

Why do I feel so compelled to write about my journey and to put into words for anyone to see my very private and personal pain?

This thing called grief is a very lonely place. It's hard to imagine that anyone else could ever have experienced this pain that I am experiencing. But I have also experienced an amazing gift through all of this, and for you to be able to know this miracle that I have witnessed, I will share my story.

My wish is that others, as unaware as I was before, will know that there is still hope. Even though you feel as though the madness is too much, just hold on. Refuse to give up on the love that you have, even though it feels so unbearable.

My wish would be that every person, every parent, every child, sibling, friend or relative would know that our loved ones are still with us, that only their physical life has changed when they die. To know that they are still here, around us, participating in our lives and communicating and loving us.

When my son Aaron was killed in a motorcycle accident, I had no knowledge of this different existence. I went through the motions of walking, eating and breathing, but that was all that I could manage for those months after Aaron's death. I would not accept that he was taken from me. I had no idea how but I was certain that I was not giving up on him. The pain and unimaginable grief was more than I could bear. Each day was worse than the previous one and each expression of condolence harder to hear. I simply thought that he was taken from me. How could that be? I was supposed to always be a mom, his mom. There to protect and care for him and his brothers. That was who I was. We were a family; his father, his brothers and me. The one thing that I knew for sure at that terrible time was that this new life now was not acceptable. This could not have happened. I kept having the same thought repeated over and over during those first few weeks: that I could find a way to fix this. I just needed time to sit and think; to figure this out, that I could find a way. When my dear friend said to me months later that her biggest fear for me was that I had no faith, it really hit home. That was so true. I had always quietly hoped that there was something else, an existence after death, but I was definitely not sold on this idea. Like many others, I found it easier just not to think about it. I was busy raising a family and enjoying every minute of life. There would be plenty of time, when I was older, to think about what happens after death. I would think about that later, not now. Well..... later was now.

I wish that I knew then what I know now. As sure as I am that I breathe and walk and love, I know that my son and all of our loved ones are still very much here with us. Why do I so completely know that this is true? Because my son Aaron made sure that I did. My story of miracles is ever changing and ongoing. The only thing that I knew for certain at that time was that I could not live without him. That simply was not an option.

My wish is that my story of miracles and love might enlighten someone else; that they might choose to investigate

X

whether there is a different existence, and that they do not have to feel as completely lost as I did. I have written about my story; as Aaron's mom as I personally experienced this journey. Each of us who knew Aaron, and were fortunate enough to experience life with him may have their own version of the miracles that he has brought forth. I know in my heart that this incredibly hard lesson which I have had to endure while here in this "Earth School" is meant to be shared with others. The accounts written in this book are true and as they happened.

Compliments of my son Aaron.

Foreward
by: Melanie May, Intuitive Medium

I am an intuitive medium. Some people aren't exactly sure what that means, and frankly, sometimes I'm not so sure either. It is truly a "blessing and a curse" as you often hear. I am extremely blessed to be able to know with unwavering doubt that there is life after death and that it is beautiful. I am blessed to experience the never-ending power of love as I communicate with spirits who have passed on. It is my belief that we are all intuitive. We come to this earth with a connection to spirit, to the universe and to something bigger than ourselves.

I have been doing private and group readings for many years now. In that time and through these experiences I have witnessed many miracles for which I am deeply grateful. But none of these experiences can quite compare to the series of events that you will read about in this book.

I vividly remember the first time I met Gayle Guadagnolo in September of 2008. It was a day that would change my life forever. I remember after Gayle had her reading I walked outside with her and her brother David. The sun was shining and it was time to say goodbye. I wanted to say "Don't go!" This was very strange to me. I have always been so grateful for my clients and love meeting so many new people. But this overwhelming urge to never let her go had never happened to me before. It is a feeling that still surfaces for me every time I am with her and it is time to leave.

Spirits, like humans, come in all sorts of shapes and sizes. Gayle's beautiful son Aaron is as big and boisterous as they come. To this day, I have never met a spirit more determined to get his messages of love and peace across to his family.

XII

Aaron has taught me so much about life and love and faith. He has helped me and thanked me and changed me for the better.

This is a story of love and grief, sorrow and joy. It is a story of Gayle's son Aaron and his unwavering love. Throughout these pages Gayle takes you to a very private, sacred place; a place hidden deep within a parent's love for a lost child. A place few of us have had to go.

I am profoundly moved by the courage it took for Gayle to write this book and put it out there for all to see. Knowing the Guadognolos has changed my life in ways I cannot even explain. I will be forever grateful to all of them and especially to Aaron.

Part I

CHAPTER ONE

Back Then

*Miracles are all around us; we just have to know
how to listen.*

I can remember life before that terrible night of Aaron's accident. Most of the days, I don't want to even think about what life will be like in the future. The saying "one day at a time" really took on new meaning. I can accept that he is not here right now, at this very minute, this hour, this day. He's been away from us before, for short periods of time, but he always came home.

I just want to go back. I want to go back to the time to when things were real, when I felt whole and complete, without this huge hole in my heart. I would do anything to go back to when we were all together as a family and I could take care of everyone. How can it be possible that I cannot take care of him now? I think of the days, the years ahead without him, and it rips at my heart more than I can imagine. It's hard to breathe.

The signs were happening. I was seeing them. I just didn't know what they meant. Life was busy. Everyone and everything was always in constant motion for us. We were just another busy family, enjoying every minute of our hectic, crazy existence. I now know that there were signs. Spring had arrived and everything and everyone was happy and cheerful. I was enjoying this great life that we were living. I was just going along like everyone else busy at being a wife and a mother to my four wonderful sons. I was fortunate to have my own business where I could set my hours around the schedule of my boys, and to work as a part-time substitute school teacher. Spring was in full swing and summertime was just around the corner.

Aaron, the second oldest of our four sons had decided to buy a motorcycle. Aaron had always done things his own way, right from the time that he was a baby and now wasn't going to be any different. We tried every possible way to change his mind when he said that he was going to buy the bike, but he was determined. I even went so far as to tell him that if he had a motorcycle, he couldn't live in our house because motorcycles were not allowed and I did not want to worry about him all of the time. Even those and other arguments of forbidding would not change his mind. He knew that we would never, under any circumstance, turn him away, but we just wanted him to reconsider and see the danger of having a motorcycle. We tried to reason with him that he would need every penny that he had saved to go back to college, but he argued that he would be saving money on gas. So, of course, he purchased the bike.

Aaron was so excited to show me the motorcycle the night that he brought it home. I don't know if it was just the protective parent in me or if I knew that something bad was going to happen. I could barely look at the bike and I definitely could not touch it. It was as if this dread came over me and I knew it right away. A motorcycle is every parent's nightmare, so I just chalked it up to "mom nerves". But I made him promise that he would drive safely on the bike, and as I walked away from it I had this almost numb feeling come over me. I couldn't figure out why I felt that way. I knew that I could not talk him out of it, that he was an adult and had purchased it without our approval. I knew in the pit of my stomach that this was not good. Maybe if I didn't look at it or touch it, the motorcycle wouldn't be there.

At about the same time that Aaron bought the bike I saw a particular commercial on television and I could not shake it from my mind. It referred to those who are lost and don't feel that they have any direction or belonging in their lives. I had never considered myself a very spiritual person and I took things more or less as they came. If I didn't like the way that something was going, it was up to me to change it. Why should it be any other way? I knew that I loved my family. My boys were my world and I knew that you had to be a good person to make a good life. For some reason however, the message of this commercial spot kept nagging at me. When I first saw it, I immediately said to myself, "How lucky I am. I know exactly where I belong in life. I am doing just what I was put here on this earth to do and that is to be a wife and the mother to my boys." In my opinion, nothing could be better and there was nothing that I wanted more. How fortunate I was to know this and to be so happy with my role in life. This was my choice and it was perfect for me. I couldn't stop thinking about that commercial though. I wondered why it was in my thoughts and how I knew that I was so sure about my life at this time. My words were replayed many, many times in my mind prior to that terrible day. I had it all. I knew that I was where I was supposed to be and I couldn't be happier.

We were having the time of our lives. It didn't get any better than this. My husband and I were just basking in the glow of a wonderful life. We enjoyed it with our four sons, took pride in their accomplishments and looked forward to the exciting future that lay ahead of them. It was now time to enjoy the ride with them as they reached adulthood, with dreams of their own. Each one of our boys was busy at the task of living life, setting his goals and accomplishing them. We were so proud of each of them. How can we be so blessed as to have a family like this? There were always a few bumps along the way, but life was so good.

Tom and I met when I was still in college. We had dated on and off for a couple of years, then drifted apart. I went to Texas with my job right after college and Tom worked in town and lived at home. I spent a couple of years working and living on my own, then decided that I wanted to be with my family. I had missed important times with my parents; my brother was starting his family and I wanted to be around. I moved myself back home with no definite plans of any kind. I wasn't home long when my Mom suggested that I give Tom a call. We had lost touch over the past couple of years and she always liked Tom. So I called him, we had a date, and that was the beginning of our life together. We were married one year later, and our first son, Kyle, arrived four days before our first wedding anniversary. Things were crazy, busy and wonderful. Our family of two grew to a family of six with the addition of each of our four sons.

Tom is a very private, quiet man. He works hard, loves his boys and me, and has always been the stable rock of our family. The boys all look up to their Dad. He has taught each one of them skills that they will always have in life. They spent time learning how to use their own hands to build things and to respect nature. The outdoors was their playground. They all hunted, fished, hiked, rode their four-wheelers, and of course played sports throughout school. Our house seemed to be the place to congregate. There were always extra friends for dinner or bodies spending the night. That was just fine with us. We wanted our boys and their friends to want to be here with us, to feel safe and welcome no matter what. I loved raising our boys. When it came time for them to go to kindergarten, I really hated to see them leave me each day and go to school. I learned, however, to appreciate the fact that they were spreading their wings. By the time that Jeffrey, our fourth son, was ready to begin school, I already had a list a mile long, of the things that I was going to do to keep busy.

As the boys grew older, each one found his passions and opportunity to excel. They all loved sports and were gifted athletes even as very young children. Lacrosse and football seemed to be their fit, although they tried every sport that they could.

They needed to be in constant motion and these two sports had it all for them. They all had a love for the outdoors and the forest, but Aaron was especially at home there. He could tell you everything and anything that had to do with the wild, the trees or nature. As a little boy he would wonder off into the woods behind our house. We would be frantic looking for him when out he would come, strutting along, bringing home all of his treasures from his expedition.

As they made their way into teenage years, our sons achieved and excelled beyond our dreams. It is such a wonderful feeling to have your children mature into young adults with such wonderful, bright futures ahead of them. Kyle and Thomas could not wait to go off to college right from the beginning. They were happy and content to be away from home. Kyle seemed to be comfortable and so self assured where ever he was. Kyle always knew what he wanted out of life and as he sets his goals he would keep his head down; working tirelessly to achieve them. It never mattered to him what everyone else was doing. He expected a lot out of himself; always striving to do his best. He is a true leader by example. Now in his senior year at Syracuse University, his incredible work ethic has never wavered and he is steadily reaching those bench marks that he has set for himself. Thomas also a student at SU, is in his freshman year. He is making his own mark in the world of collegiate lacrosse and following right on the heels of his older brother. Thomas and Kyle resemble each other very much physically and in their personalities, yet Kyle is more serious and more focused of the two. Thomas excels in most everything that he pursues, however he also lends plenty of time to his social life and social planning. Thomas always seems to be in the middle of the action and enjoying it to the fullest. It didn't take him long at all to establish his new family at school and be very comfortable there. Kyle and Thomas seemed tailor made for the college scene; eager to let loose and to be on their own. Who knows how Jeffrey, only fifteen will emerge. He's busy trying to fill those amazingly big shoes that his three older brothers have left in his path and at the same time fulfill his own dreams. Aaron, however, was another story. He wasn't so sure of what he wanted to do. He wanted to be in college and knew it was the correct path to further his opportunities, but he wasn't one for being away from home. He gave it a try.

The first time that I dropped him off at college and settled him in, he actually returned home before I did. Sometimes we would wake up in the morning, thinking that he was supposed to be at school, only to find him home in his own bed. Who would have expected that, when you looked at this massive man-child?

Aaron was always the big guy. By the time he was sixteen, he was six foot, two inches tall, and two hundred pounds. Once he reached the age of ten, he never really looked like a little boy, but deep in his heart, he was the biggest kid of all. He loved to have fun, kid around and to be home. When Aaron was a little boy, he would come home from school and he would try to tell you everything about the day in one sentence. He bounced up and down as he spoke, so excited about his day. This enthusiasm of his wasn't always his best friend and there were many phone calls and notes from school personnel, politely asking for help to contain some of his energy. As he got older, his zest for life never changed. He did, however, become better at navigating the backlash. I would always say that he was like the town mayor; he could talk his way in or out of anything.

Aaron spent the majority of his time outdoors enjoying nature. That is where he was most comfortable. He was always doing something in the woods or scouting for game. Jeffrey, the youngest of the four boys, seems to have been born with the same passion and love for the outdoors and nature as Aaron. He and Aaron were always on the same page when it came to hunting and the woods. Aaron took Jeffrey under his wing and was eager to teach him all that he could about their favorite pastime. It wasn't long before Jeffrey was right there side-by-side with his brother. It's hard as the youngest of the four boys, not to be completely influenced by his older brothers, but Jeffrey seems to be a combination of them all, with his own self-awareness and his own confidence. He definitely is his own person, on his own path with his dreams starting to emerge.

CHAPTER TWO

Spring 2008

Springtime was here. We were so busy just enjoying every minute. Where had the time gone? The warm days were becoming more frequent. We were approaching the final semester of school and graduation for Kyle. Both Kyle and Thomas played on the men's lacrosse team at Syracuse University and Aaron had also been a student and member of that team the previous year. Aaron's time at Syracuse University was probably some of the happiest of his life. He felt as though he had really found his niche there; at least socially. He was everyone's brother at SU. It didn't take him any time at all to know everyone and for them to know him. He was your big brother, your best friend and he always had your back.

On one occasion, while all of us except Aaron were away at a lacrosse tournament, I happened to learn that a huge party was taking place at our house. The guest list included many of the athletes and students from SU as well as many of Aaron's friends from our small town. That was Aaron's specialty. He brought people from all different walks of life and all different ages together. They were all his friends. You could be old enough to be his father or grandfather, but when you were with him he made you feel ageless, just one of the guys. However, academics and studies were not his focus at the time, so he was taking some time off from school. He was living at home and working with his Dad while planning what to do next with his future.

While Aaron and Jeffrey; a sophomore in high school, were living at home, Kyle and Thomas were wrapping up the school year and the college lacrosse season at Syracuse. And what a year of lacrosse it turned out to be. The whole season had a magical aura to it and everyone felt it. Everything that they had worked so hard for was paying off. They just seemed to have all of the elements of a championship team. The anticipation of earning that golden ticket in the arena of college lacrosse was within their grasp.

At last the final season playoff game had been won and we were so excited to be off for the grand stage of college lacrosse; the final four games and hopefully the National Championship games. All of the preparations were in the works as we could hardly wait for Thursday to get here. We would all be going to support our boys, Kyle, Thomas and the whole SU team. We were so busy planning. Everything was in a fast forward mode. We had less than one week from the time of the final playoff game to the championship venue. Syracuse lacrosse has long had a tradition of massive tailgating participation and this would be on an even grander scale. It would be no easy undertaking. The parents and supporters would all band together and no doubt pull off our usual orange and blue party in the parking lot. We were making hotel reservations, securing event tickets for all of us and organizing one massive party. The phones were constantly ringing, emails were going back and forth and we were getting it done, all the while in a state of "pinch me" excitement.

CHAPTER THREE

Tuesday, May 20, 2008

It was just another busy night in our house and we were off to another lacrosse game, which is what we seem to do in the spring. All four boys play lacrosse. Some years we would have a child on each of the modified, JV and Varsity lacrosse teams. Now with Kyle and Thomas playing on the same team for SU, we only had to balance their games on the weekends and Jeffrey's Varsity games during the week. We were getting ready to leave for Jeffrey's game, and I went down stairs to say good- bye to Aaron as he was getting ready to go out. He was standing at the bathroom sink; talking on the phone while at the same time brushing his teeth. "How can you do that?" I asked. But, that was Aaron. I said that we were going to the high school and told him to be careful when he went out.

We were just returning home from Jeffrey's game. Tom was checking the emails on the computer and I was getting Jeffrey something to eat. The phone rang and a voice that I could not recognize said, "Gayle put Tom on the phone." I thought it was a little strange, but gave the phone to Tom.

Life as we knew it, ended in that moment. Aaron, our 21 year old son, had been killed in a motorcycle accident. THIS WAS NOT HAPPENING! THERE WAS NO WAY THIS WAS HAPPENING!

He had just gone out. He had just gotten the bike. Why did we let him go? Why didn't we stop him from leaving the house that night? Why didn't I tell him how much I loved him before he left?

There had to be a way to fix this. We could always find a way to fix anything. That's what we did; we were his parents. There had to be a way......

When the call came that there had been an accident, to hurry and go to the scene, I had a calm feeling come over me that it would be fine. It would be just another scare, like so many that we had experienced while raising four active boys. We were always taking someone in for stitches or to the emergency room. This, too, would be okay. Aaron, the second oldest of our four boys, was a big, strong guy. Nothing really bad could happen to him. He was a fireman; he helped people all of the time. It wasn't even an option. He was just going out for ice cream with his friend on their new motorcycles.

We went to the scene. It seemed as if I wasn't really there, that I was observing from a distance. I didn't break through the arms holding me back and run to where he was. I stayed at a distance. Why? That was not like me. That was my son lying there. At the hospital, when the doctors and nurses just stared at me with horrified eyes, I couldn't imagine what they were trying to say to me. They must be talking to someone else.

Why did I allow them to say those words to me? Why didn't I take you into my arms and get us out of there? But I didn't. I'm not sure if I was saying the words out loud or just over and over in my mind. I was begging you to get up.

Let's go home. Let's get out of here. We don't belong here. We can go home now, and I will take care of everything, of you. Just get up!

The next thing that I remember is looking up and seeing so many people all lined up inside the hospital room. Who were these men and women? Where did they all come from?

They were crying and I couldn't help them. Everything seemed to be happening in slow motion. Tom was trying to telephone Kyle and Thomas, who were at school; Jeffrey was with us. At one point Jeffrey asked if everyone could leave him alone with Aaron. He said that he had some things to say to him. How did he become so strong, so mature at fifteen? I am so grateful that Jeffrey will always have the memory of those special moments with his brother.

I can remember standing there, feeling as if I were surrounded by a heavy, dense matter that held me up. I guess that they must have told us that it was time to leave now.

Why didn't I insist that you get up and come home with us? How could I leave you there?

This definitely is not what I would have done. Nobody else took care of my kids; that was my job. I always took care of them. Why wasn't I doing that now? I had never left him alone, not once in twenty-one years. Why didn't I stamp my feet, throw a fit; refuse to leave him? Instead, I just seemed to float along and do what they told me to do. For the life of me, I can't figure out why I gave up so easily and we went home without him. Where was I? Why didn't I fight? Why couldn't I stop this chaos? Why didn't I make this all right?

I wanted no part of the events that followed. I wanted him only for myself, for Tom and for his brothers. Why did any plans have to be made? This didn't concern anyone but us and I couldn't breathe. I thought that if I looked long and hard enough, into the woods behind our house, the woods that Aaron loved so much, then everything would go back to how it was supposed to be. I thought that I would see him coming along. With that undeniable bouncing gait of his, out of the pine trees towards the house swinging his arms and just looking around at everything that he loved. Aaron absolutely loved the outdoors. He absorbed anything that had to do with wildlife, the outdoors, hunting or fishing. He took after my Dad in that respect. He and Aaron would talk endlessly about their favorite topics. You could just see it in Aaron's total being that he lived for the outdoors. That was his classroom; that was his church.

I didn't see him come out of the woods, no matter how hard I tried. I didn't dare look away and I still search there many times each day. All of this has been so strange, so foreign. There are times when I just want to run, to run away anywhere as fast as I can, just to keep ahead of all this madness. And then I think: how can I leave the woods? What if I can't look for him?

As we reeled from this unbelievable nightmare, life was still going on around us, even though we couldn't see how that was possible. More decisions, hard, impossible ones had to be made. They were difficult, not just for Tom and me, but for all of us. When I seemed to crumble the most, my children showed such strength and character. To me they are just little boys who need me to protect and guide them. When did they become such wonderful young men? Not only did Kyle and Thomas have this heartache of the loss of their brother, they also had to make the decision whether or not to travel with their lacrosse team and fight for the national championship. Their team would be leaving the next day. The games were in Boston on Memorial Day weekend. For many people, this decision would be a simple one. They don't know the character of my boys. Kyle knew that as a captain and key defensive player on the team his presence or absence would have a definite impact on the outcome of the games. Even though their hearts were breaking, this was their team. How could they let them down? They had worked so hard to get to these games.

Kyle and Thomas knew how excited we all were about

going to the championships.   Aaron had been excited too and couldn't wait to go along with the rest of us and cheer his brothers on to certain victory.   The absence of Kyle and Thomas would be felt by the team.   Playing in these championship games would bring back some meaning to their world that had been devastated.   As long as it was okay with their dad and me they would go, and bring it home for the team and for Aaron.

Chapter Four

Courage

I could not believe what was happening. Aaron was supposed to be here with us; cracking his jokes, making his plans, living his life. How can all of that end with such finality and in a split second? How can anyone accept this? I couldn't. I was looking for the answer; a way to undo what had occurred. My mind was reeling yet at the same time, I felt so numb as though I could not finish a complete thought.

As I look back now to the way in which things were unfolding, I realize that even then this journey was on a path all of its own. I had the brakes on full force and I was not giving Aaron up. I knew in my heart that there had to be a way that I could fix this but I didn't know how. I had to figure it out. I couldn't think. I could not move ahead with anything or any plans. I needed time. I couldn't breathe.

The next several days went by in a blur. Two days after Aaron's accident Kyle and Thomas went to Boston, along with a massive collection of adoptive parents who took them under their wings. Tom and I knew that as hard as it was to do so, we could entrust this extended family with our precious sons. Tom was so torn. Kyle and Thomas' dream of winning a national championship was also Tom's dream. What parent wouldn't want to share in such glory with their sons? All of the boys were very involved in sports and we had never missed a game. Sometimes it meant splitting the duties and each of us went in different directions. Sometimes it meant recruiting a grandparent or other relative to stand in for us when there were more activities than the two of us could physically attend. We were always there for them. What should Tom do? The boys wanted him and needed him with them, but he felt that he had to be with us at home. With plenty of family and friends for support, Jeffrey and I would be just fine. Kyle and Thomas said that they understood if Tom didn't go, but they were desperately hoping that he would show up. Tom felt as though he was abandoning his boys, but he also felt responsible to take care of things at home, and his heart was completely broken. It was all so surreal.

Friday; the day after Kyle and Thomas left for Boston we learned that Tom's father would have to undergo immediate open-heart surgery. The surgery would take place the following day. Without this surgery, he might not survive the weekend. Tom's dad had always gone to all of the boys' games with us. He became one of the teams' resident Gramps. The weekend before, at the final season playoff game, he had complained slightly of a pain in his shoulder and he seemed to have some difficulty keeping up with everyone as we walked the distances to the stadiums.

This was so much to handle. Why? Why now? What could we possibly have done to have all of this happen to us? Could Tom handle any more stress? Lord knows, most of the burden was falling on him. I was so deep in my own sorrow that I couldn't help him. I simply was not accepting any of this.

Kyle and Thomas had arrived in Boston with their team. They had completed a day of practice on Friday and were now waiting anxiously for Saturday; the day of the first eliminating games for the final four teams. We had decided not to tell the boys about their Grandfather's condition and his scheduled surgery. We would wait until after the game and the surgery so that they could celebrate two victories.

Saturday morning arrived. It was the day of the final four game; the day of surgery for Tom's Dad and another day in our new lives with our hearts broken. The phones were ringing like crazy as family and friends were starting to arrive at our house. Tom was a wreck. He was so worried about his Dad. He was worried about Kyle and Thomas. He was worried about Jeffrey and me. The team parents and our friends kept us constantly informed on how our boys were holding up. We were told of the many ways in which friends, teammates, fans and people that we didn't even know were honoring our boys and Aaron. We were so happy for their success and so proud of them. But how could I smile? I was in complete agony. I felt so guilty that I truly could not share in the happiness for my sons. All I could feel was pain.

We had a large crowd at home with us, watching the game, cheering them on in traditional "Guad Squad" fashion. But what was the point, I wondered? How could everyone look at the television and pretend to care about a game, when my heart was aching? I just wanted to scream. I know that everyone was trying to help, to live in that moment if only for Kyle and Thomas.

There were always so many of the Guadagnolo family and friends at all of the games that we had decided to form our own cheering section, and we all sported tee shirts bragging "The Guad Squad". Aaron's tee shirt was given an honorary place on the team bench during the final four and championship games. It was an emotional start on Saturday, but the team won their game; earning them one of the two positions in the championship game to be played in two days which would be on Memorial Day. Now, Kyle and Thomas had achieved their dream; a chance to play in the national championship lacrosse game. When Kyle was a little boy he used to ask if we thought the he would ever be good enough to play lacrosse in college. There was never any doubt.

Syracuse won the final four playoff game. The team was now on its way to the championship game. We learned later that same Saturday afternoon that Tom's father had survived his open-heart surgery and was doing well. Now Tom could put the worry of his father's illness behind him as he tried to cope with everything else that was going on.

Kyle and Thomas were proud of the win but they were still in agony over Aaron's death and in need of us. As Tom struggled with what he should do, where he should be, the decision was made quite clear with a little advice from a dear friend: "Just do what your heart tells you." Well, that's all we needed to hear. Tom started packing and phone calls were made. Off to Boston he went with his brother- in- law Wayne. Wayne helped Tom hold it all together. Never in his life, he later told me, did he know how right a decision had been than when he saw the faces of Kyle and Thomas. Their world was turned upside down, yet they had a job to do and they needed their dad.

At the end of the day victory prevailed. Of course they won the Championship Lacrosse game on Memorial Day. They were now national champions. Not one of them doubted that they would win. You could ask any SU player that day and he would have said that losing wasn't even on the table. They wouldn't have it any other way, nor would Aaron. He gave strength to those players that day and unimaginable courage to his brothers. The opposing team didn't have a chance of winning.

The celebration of their accomplishment was so wonderful and the pain was so raw. How can you possibly handle these two very opposite, very extreme emotions at the same time? Our boys, our family and our friends all had to balance this thrill and this heartache. Their joy was so short-lived, as each one knew that as they left that stadium and that atmosphere of celebration the next days would be so hard. They never faltered, not one of them. They were there to support their brothers, their teammates, their friends. With the love and support of all of our families and friends we got through the next days together. No one could do this alone.

Chapter Five

Don't Let Me Forget

On the day that we buried you my friend told me that she will never forget watching me looking at you, not able to take my eyes off of you. I kept looking at you as we walked away and left you there.

How did I leave you there? It's as though I was floating through time, like it wasn't even me. If I really were there, I never would have left you. I had to burn that image of you into my mind. I couldn't accept that this would be it, the last time to see you. My brain was so numb, yet I was trying so desperately to somehow drink in every bit of you, so that I could maybe take you with me and keep this from going any further. I wanted to stop everything and everyone. Please, don't let me forget.

Throughout those terrible days we learned again and again just how much Aaron was loved by so many people. I knew that he was wonderful, but did I truly understand how magnificent he really was? Was I so busy raising him that I might have missed out on the JOY of him, the joy that others experienced with him? You can't get back those precious moments and you don't know what you've missed until it's too late and you can't have them. It scares me so much to think that maybe I might have missed even the smallest detail of him. I don't want to have missed one smile, one word or one sparkle of life from him. If only we could go back in time; I'd change so many things.

I thought that I understood the importance of loving your family and being the best parent that you can be. I wish that

I knew before, what I know now. I would have sat Aaron down, held his face in my hands, looked him straight in the eye and I would have told him again and again how much I loved him. I would have told him over and over how wonderful and special he was. I would never have let him leave my sight without making sure that he knew without a doubt that I will love him always. I had told him all the time that I loved him. I thought that he knew, but was I sure that he really understood how much he was loved? Would he know for eternity if I never got the chance to tell him again? Did I take the time to really make sure that he knew that, above all else? I would have made certain that he knew that, even though there were times that we didn't see things the same way, those things didn't matter. What was important is that Aaron knew that he was loved unconditionally. That was my job, my most important job with all of my boys: to always be there to let them know how much I loved them and to reassure them that everything would be okay. If they were feeling unsure or sad, I could make them feel better. Now, in just the blink of an eye, Aaron is not there. I'm not able to do what I was put here on this earth to do: to take care of him, soothe his fears, and make him feel safe. Never could I have imagined not being able to take care of my child, to make sure that he is okay, to be his mom. This is such a feeling of complete emptiness.

The hours, days and weeks that followed were a time of merely existing, nothing more. How could this have happened? Why? He was too young; it was too soon; we needed more time with him. Who wrote these rules of life anyway? This was so unfair. He needed his Dad and me, and we needed him.

CHAPTER SIX

Signs From Aaron

And so, began this amazing journey of love……

As a fog started to settle in on us, we found ourselves existing in a different world. Although our grief may have been clouding our eyesight, our miracle of miracles was beginning to make its presence known. I never could have imagined how alone and lost that I could feel. I had Tom, Kyle, Thomas and Jeffrey, but our family was no longer whole without Aaron. I had no faith or true belief on which I could rely. I had always hoped that there was something more after you died. However, I really wasn't sure if I believed that or not. Sometimes I would try to believe, but more often I felt that I was wishing for the impossible. I had myself convinced that this was it, yet all the while I prayed that there was more. My heart was so heavy. This was my son. How could he have gone away? He can't leave us behind. I made so many deals with and pleas to who-ever that Greater Power might be, to do whatever was needed to just bring him back. We all needed Aaron here. How could it be possible that he is no more?

The summer after Aaron's death was one big blur. We were going through the motions of trying to do what was right and what needed to be done. Our boys were trying to pick up the pieces and to continue their lives. Tom and I were not much more than two injured bodies. We tried to breathe, we tried to live, but most of the time that was asking the impossible.

Our hurt was so all-consuming that we hardly noticed anything else. But the signs were beginning to present themselves, whether we noticed them or not. I would often sit on our deck that overlooks our back yard. More often than not, a blue heron would either be there when I came out or would show up shortly thereafter. This bird would appear in our yard and usually come to the side closest to the deck. He would just sit there and sit there, regardless if I made noise, movements or anything else. How odd I thought, that this bird would turn its head and just look at me for what seemed to be very long periods of time. As I would sit and think, with tears streaming down my face, this blue heron would stay and not look away. I came to expect that the bird to be there when I went out. It gave me a little comfort.

I kept telling Tom also during these first few months that I needed a year: I just needed a year to sit and think and not have to talk to anyone. I didn't really have any idea of why I thought that I needed a year, or how I knew that I needed a year, but it was constantly on my mind. I could not make any sense of this loss.

I kept thinking and asking myself, "How can we fix this? There has to be something that we can do. I cannot and will not settle for this. Aaron is our son; he is supposed to be here with us. He's mine; you can't have him." I would find myself sitting for hours, then, wondering how I had gotten there. I could participate in some things. It seemed, though, that only half of my mind would show up; the other half was off in this terrible place called grief.

About three months after Aaron's death, a friend asked me if I would talk to someone that she knew who had lost her son the previous year. I knew that I was sinking fast, so I was

willing to listen to anyone, once.   Laura came to my house
and I could not believe her courage. This beautiful woman
sat at my table and told me about the heartbreaking loss of
her only son, Jay. I was shocked that she could talk about
him the way that she did, so sweet and controlled. Didn't she
realize that her son was gone from her? How could she sit
and talk of him with this peaceful way about her and actually
say his name, without completely falling apart and crying her
eyes out? I was in disbelief. I could not even think about
Aaron or say his name, even in my mind, without crumbling.
How could she do this? She said that even though she missed
her son Jay, she knew that he was always around her. His
spirit was ever present and active in her life. She knew this
because she had gone to see a medium. This medium, Laura
said, was so gifted and had told her things about her son, inti-
mate and personal validations. She had told her things that no
one except Laura and Jay could have known. This medium
told Laura that this information and these validations were
brought to her from her son Jay so that she would trust that
he is always with her and that he loves her.

"Well, maybe it worked for you, but it is never going to
work for me", was all that I could say. Those were my exact
thoughts and words. As I said, I had never had much faith
nor did I spend much time thinking about death and what
happens after we die, until Aaron died. Years ago, some family members had gone to see a psychic at the State Fair. My
mother had always been a big believer in psychics and the
spiritual world, but I was never drawn to it. I had read a
couple of books by well known authors on the subject.   I
found them very entertaining and intriguing, but that was as
far as my interests went. I really didn't know the difference
between a psychic and a medium. So we all went in a group
and each had a turn to listen and be read by these psychic/

palm readers. When my turn came, I was determined not to give away any information whatsoever; to let the psychic do all of the telling. As I walked into the room where a psychic waited and sat down, my mother was having her reading in the adjacent room by another psychic. They were talking on and on and she was giving my Mom all kinds of information. When I sat for my reading, the woman looked at my palms and said, "There is nothing to say to you. There is nothing to say." Well, that was weird. I thought about it for a short while then I just assumed that it was me; that I couldn't be read and that was that. Now when I think back about that experience, I wonder whether there really wasn't anything to say to me, or whether the psychic saw something that she didn't want to convey.

After Laura told me about her experiences with the medium and her son, I just couldn't stop thinking about it. I knew that Laura had lived through what I was experiencing and that she truly believed what she told me. This could not be some cruel joke. Her pain was still so raw and obvious, yet she was so sure and matter- of- fact that her son was still with her. Could this possibly be true? Could I find Aaron? Is this why I simply refused to give up? I was much more desperate now and I was willing to contemplate any possibility if I could only get him back. I desperately wanted what she said to be true; I would give anything for it to be true. I needed him back. But how do I do that? How do I start my search? What if I can't find my son?

I finally made the phone call. I called to schedule my own appointment with this medium. The first time that I called, I hung up when the phone was answered. I was really scared. I felt as though I was making the biggest leap of faith imaginable. I was putting everything out there on the line. I was taking the biggest risk of my entire life. I knew that this was it for me. If what Laura said was true about this medium, my life would change again in a moment. If it wasn't true, then I would be no worse off and would continue to live in this horrible haze. If I could only find out whether Aaron was okay, it would mean so much. As I saw it, there was no other choice to be made. I had nothing to lose. It couldn't get any worse than this.

I told only my husband Tom and my brother David about this. David's daughter, Jennifer, had passed away from cancer nine years before Aaron's death. Not only did David have to live with the devastating death of his daughter, but he also had to live with the burden that he had been responsible for making all of the decisions concerning her care. No matter what they tried, there was no stopping the spread of Jennifer's disease. As painful as it is to live with the death of your child, I can't imagine living with that too. So I asked David if he would want to go with me to see this medium. I had no idea how he had been able to live with Jennifer's absence for so long. I knew in my heart that if he could get some answers and relief from this medium, then this risk would be well worth it. He deserved more than anyone to hear from his daughter, after years of missing her so. I also knew that by putting the emphasis on him; I took some of the pressure off my own fears. David agreed to see the medium with me.

Off we went with our hearts on our sleeves. As we drove to our appointments David was trying to gently warn me that my prayers might not be answered that day as I was hoping. We were both trying to control our overwhelming feeling of "wanting so badly to hear from Jennifer and Aaron" by giving "keep calm, don't get your hopes up" speeches to each other. I didn't know that David had done this before. He had visited other spiritual healers and mediums, with no real heart-lifting success. But, he was willing to give it a try again, for my sake and his. How could you not do anything in your power, go to any length, to get some part of your child back?

We arrived for our scheduled appointments. I would go first. I felt as though I was going through a door and would never be able to go back. This would be it. That's when I met Melanie May.

CHAPTER SEVEN

I Sent The Big Bird

As Melanie May greeted us at her office, I knew in that first instant that this woman would never do anything to hurt anyone, including us. She definitely was not what I had pictured. I think that David and I both had "the whole gypsy thing" going on in our minds and we couldn't have been more wrong. Melanie was this very sweet, friendly, compassionate, young, beautiful woman who could be anyone's sister. Wow! That was a relief. This was definitely looking better.

I had scheduled a forty-five minute reading with Melanie thinking that surely this would be more than enough time. I also didn't want the silence of her not being able to read me, to drag on for too long. I was rather sure that again there would be nothing for the medium to say to me. I was wrong again.

Melanie May is an intuitive medium and she is clairsentient. This means that she is clear feeling. Melanie feels things from those who have passed and gets communications from them. She feels physically and emotionally what the spirits had experienced and what we experience. Sometimes spirits bring to her the manner in which they passed or what they went through in life. It's difficult enough to deal with your own issues and problems, but Melanie also experiences these things with others. She does this to pass along the validating information to you, so that you know that what she is telling you is true. She immediately started telling me things from my son Aaron that she could not possibly have known on her own. She said things that were very current and that only I could know.

One of the first things that Aaron mentioned was to thank Laura. Aaron did not know her in life, but he wanted to thank her for what she had done. I knew immediately who he was talking about. Laura is the beautiful woman that came to my house and told me about Melanie. Laura lost her son Jay the year before Aaron's accident. Aaron told us that he was with Jay as he mentioned him by name. I was completely speechless. Melanie told me next that Aaron said that he had sent the big bird; the blue heron that constantly showed up at my house since his accident. My mind was racing to connect to everything that she was telling me from Aaron. Sometimes I couldn't keep up. My heart was pounding with all of this confirming information from him and at the same time I was trying to grasp that he truly was still with me. Never before in my life had I experienced such joy.

It had happened to me again. In an instant my life was completely changed. I truly thought that life with Aaron as part of it in it had ceased to exist. Now I knew that he was with me. It certainly was not the way that I would have chosen, but for now I would take any way that I could get. I was in a complete daze when I walked out of my reading with Melanie. I remember so clearly that when my reading with her was finished, she said to me, "You know, you don't need me; he's there." Who was she kidding!! I just wanted to take her home with me or go home with her. I knew that there would be so many things that I would want to ask her and that I would definitely be back to see her often.

David went in for his reading after me. The only words of encouragement that I could speak to him when I came out were, "You'll never believe it." I immediately called Tom and told him all of the things that Aaron had said and passed along the messages that he had specifically for his Dad. This entire event was even more out of Tom's comfort zone than it was out of mine, and he was quite stunned.

Tom had carved a beautiful plaque which read "Aaron's Forest" and had made the posts for it out of a special tree that Aaron liked. Tom had placed this labor of love in our woods, behind our house to honor Aaron's memory. Aaron had told Melanie that he was standing by the plaque and the special tree. He said that he had been with Tom when he was making it and described the tree in detail. No one knew about this. How could this be? Aaron also brought up the fact that he was with me as I read each night. I was reading anything that I could find, trying to make some sense out of it all. There were parts in the books that I skipped because I felt that they didn't pertain to me. I was concerned that by skipping over some parts I might not get the "whole picture" and that I might be missing something important. These specific thoughts went through my mind but were never spoken out loud. Aaron said that it was okay to skip the parts in the book that did not feel right. He told Melanie his first and middle name, as well as his friends' names. He talked about the little boy Junior, who was his girlfriend's three year old brother. He spoke of his brothers and gave so many specific validations that would have meaning only to me. He really was there. My heart was soaring. I couldn't believe how I could go from the lowest of low to this feeling of hope again.

I taped my session that day. I consider that tape recording to be one of my most valued treasures. This was my link, my lifeline to my son. I wanted so badly to listen to the tape, but I didn't want to listen to it without Tom. What if something happened to the tape upon playing it? I couldn't take the chance that Tom would not hear Melanie's words from

Aaron for himself. Tom, however, was not yet ready to listen. Each time that we would try to listen, he would say "Turn it off; not now". I patiently waited, truly understanding that it had to be the right time for him. I wouldn't listen without him, but when he was ready we would play the recording.

As time went on, we realized that he just wasn't going to be ready any time soon. Tom convinced me to go ahead and listen to the tape by myself. I reluctantly, yet eagerly, played the tape. When I first listened to the replay, I was floored.

My friend Linda and I were driving in my car and listening to the session. On the tape, over Melanie's words and blocking her voice for just a split second, there came the sound of a man's voice that said "Mom". Neither one of us said anything at first, but both of us heard it. We tried to remain calm and kept playing the tape recording. The man's voice was there again, this time even more clear; "Mom". Well, it was hard to sit, let alone drive the car down the highway. I felt sure that I was imagining it. This couldn't be real. It was my mind playing a trick; making me hear what I so desperately wanted to hear. I listened to the tape again and again. No, it was definitely there: "Mom"

David had gone in for his reading immediately following mine. When he came out I saw that he was pretty much in a daze, just as I had been. Neither of us could seem to get many words out; our heads and hearts were reeling. When David sat down with Melanie, the first thing that she told him was that there was an older gentleman who was always there for David and that he was on our father's side of the family. This man said that he looked out for David. When David had gone to other mediums and psychics some of them had also mentioned this same older man watching over him. Melanie continued to describe this man and his role in David's life. Although David was intrigued and happy to hear this validation, he was patiently waiting to hear from the one person that his heart was aching for: his daughter Jennifer. Finally, Jen made her presence known. When her spirit appeared to Melanie, she immediately recognized Jennifer. Melanie told David that when she was giving her first reading of that day to a man just before we arrived, a young girl kept coming forward in that reading. Melanie would bring information to her client, but the information was not making any sense to him and he couldn't make the connection. Finally, Melanie told this young girl's spirit that she knew how excited she was. However, it was not her turn yet and she would have to wait. Well, if you knew Jennifer, you would know how she would respond if she were reprimanded. If someone had said that she was going ahead of her turn or was being too pushy, then she definitely would have shrunk back and waited until she was invited to participate. It made perfect sense why she waited so quietly for David's reading to progress. She didn't even come forward during my reading. She left the entire session for Aaron.

David had waited so many years for this moment that I think that it was really hard for him to accept that it was for real. He kept telling himself that if only she said the one phrase that he was waiting to hear, then he would definitely know that it was Jen. She never did say the words that he was waiting for in his reading. Even though he did hear many other validations, he had his heart set on "the Bunny". That's all that he wanted to hear. When Jennifer was so sick she kept with her as her comfort companion a blue bunny that she named Floppy. David said that he wasn't giving up. He would keep asking her to someday, somehow say those words.

When we got into the car after our readings, we were both rather quiet. We were trying to absorb and remember what had been said. David told me about the gentleman who came through in his reading. He asked me if I knew anyone on our Dad's side of the family who had his toes or foot cut off. That was the information that the gentleman had brought to Melanie to identify himself which Melanie relayed to David. He said that his name was Joe. Did I know any relative by that name? I had no idea and had never heard of any such story or relative. When David got back to his office, he told our father about our experience that morning. He was going to ask our Dad whether he knew of any relatives by the name of Joe. Our father immediately said, even before David could finish, "That was my uncle, but they called him "Toke", and he had his foot cut off because of diabetes." David couldn't believe what our dad was saying. No one had ever told either of us that story and Joe ("Toke") had passed long before either David or I was born.

The miracles just kept coming. The thing about my family is that we come as a package deal. It seems that if you know one of us, you get all of us. It's always been that way. Of course all of my family and many of Aaron's friends wanted to hear from him as well. I relayed to anyone who would listen the miracle of messages from my son. Every couple of days, though, I would convince myself that I was making this all up, that I heard what I wanted to hear. I would listen again to the taped sessions and I could breathe again. I couldn't wait to hear from another one of our family members or friends who had been to see Melanie. Each time they would receive validations and confirmations from Aaron that were meaningful and current in their lives, yet so life-saving for me.

My existence was measured by who was going next, for a reading with Melanie May. I felt as though I had discovered that the earth was round, as though this was something that came to life just because I would not give up on Aaron. I had no idea that this beautiful continuation of love really existed. Where had I been for the first fifty years of my life? How had I existed without this awareness before? I know as surely as I know that my heart is beating, that this newfound love from my son Aaron has saved my life.

CHAPTER EIGHT

Messages From Aaron

Aaron's personality and physical stature were bigger than life itself. A big presence right from birth, Aaron stood six foot, three, with a massive body and an outgoing personality to match. Somehow you knew that Aaron had arrived even before he walked into the room. Being the second born of our four boys, he was also the free spirit of the family. Aaron had a way of turning every situation into something to laugh about. He didn't take too many things seriously and could always find a way to infuse humor and fun into most situations.

From the time that he was a little boy it was always full speed ahead with Aaron. He saw only that he needed to get from point A to point B, and didn't see anything in between. Sometimes this didn't work out in his favor. It didn't matter if you were young or old he made you feel as if you were his best friend and you could always be yourself with him. If he was your friend, you got all of him: his crazy passions, his sense of humor, his complete self. There was no holding back with Aaron; he came in one big, here I am huggable package. Aaron lived his life that way from the moment that he was born. He was one big ball of activity from the moment his eyes opened until the moment that his head hit the pillow. He always had a million things going all at the same time. He knew his way around everywhere and he knew everyone wherever he went. He could easily bring out the extremes of my personality: I would be as furious as could be with him, and want to laugh and hug him all in the same moment. That was Aaron. That's what is now missing from my heart. How thrilled we were to find that Aaron's spirit was all around us, never faltering, and with no intention of going away. This knowledge alone became our lifeline, gently pulling us back to the reality of life when the hurt became too great.

Melanie May can talk to the spirits. I know now that we all can communicate with them to some degree, if we really want to do so. But she has a gift like no other. She can actually carry on a conversation, ask questions, get answers and even articulate the personalities of the spirits of our loved ones. Melanie delivers these messages with more love and compassion than I ever knew one person could possess. She has a second gift as well as her gift of intuition: the wonderful ability to put you at ease and convey every ounce of love that is coming from those we miss so much. Any apprehension or uneasiness is left behind as she begins this journey of reconnection for you.

Some spirits have an easier time communicating with Melanie than others. Aaron, she says, is one of the strongest and clearest who communicates with her and he has become a big part of her life. Who would have guessed? So the continuation of messages from Aaron that everyone was receiving through Melanie were not surprising, nor were we surprised at how quickly and undeniably Aaron made himself such a special part of Melanie's life too. She never knew in advance when someone connected to Aaron was coming to see her and it never took her long to realize just who had shown up for the meeting. He would so clearly and lovingly remind each of us that he was always with us and involved in our daily lives. Sometimes Aaron would hold back his identity from Melanie, so that the person there for the reading would be able to trust that the messages truly were from him. Melanie would be amazed as he would finally reveal himself. It was so clever of him to go to such lengths to disguise himself or to hold back. Aaron, always the prankster, has not changed. Even though we cannot physically see him, he still teases and plays jokes on each of us, just as before. The only difference is that now we have to be a little more open to recognize the signs; they are still there.

All of our readings with Melanie have been incredible. Each of us would come away with a renewed sense of hope and maybe a little more understanding of this tragedy of Aaron's death. Each reading was pure love and magic for our hearts. Friends and family taped their sessions with Melanie. I've listened to the tapes afterwards. While listening I would feel like I was wrapped in a blanket of "Aaron-ness".

When my sister-in law went for her reading, Aaron came through with messages again that affected us all. The week before Cheri's reading some members of our family and friends had attended a remembrance Mass in honor of Aaron. We went up together to light a candle for him. This was a very emotional event for all of us; it was difficult to see through our tears.

Aaron however, would have thought that the whole thing was really "lame", but I'm sure that a side of him would also have appreciated the effort. During Cheri's reading Aaron thanked her for going to the service for him. Then he laughed because we had problems lighting the candle for him; it would not light. He thought that this was very funny and said that he had caused the problem. Cheri thought that I had lit the candle and asked me if I had had any trouble in my attempts to light it. "I didn't even light the candle. It was Tom who lit it". I told her. Tom had not mentioned anything about that night to me, so I asked him if anything had happened when he was lighting the candle. Tom said "I couldn't get the candle to light for anything. Each time I would try to light it, it would blow right out. I almost said "forget it". I was really starting to get pissed".

That was Aaron. He could always push our buttons just enough and then make you laugh at him, all in the same moment. It was his specialty and it was one of the things that we didn't realize that we loved so much about him. He hadn't lost his touch.

"I was there at the party. Check the pictures." This was the next message that Aaron relayed during Cheri's reading. A surprise anniversary party was held for Tom and me, to celebrate our 25th anniversary. A group of relatives and friends, both ours and Aaron's, had gathered at the home of Tom's sister and brother-in-law; Mary and Wayne. They made a very beautiful event out of a day that neither Tom nor I felt like celebrating. We were so grateful for the thoughtfulness of all of these people. Every effort imaginable was made to ensure a wonderful day, yet it hung in the air, a feeling that someone was undeniably missing. Some of the people at the party had taken pictures during that day, so I made it my mission to find the photographers and their pictures. Would Aaron show himself as we knew him in the pictures? Surely, if that were the case someone would have noticed it in the pictures by now. We searched each picture of that day. Could that be him? What? Where? We looked for the subtle and the obvious, with no luck. Why couldn't we find him? I was so disappointed, but I was not giving up.

Thanksgiving Day was approaching and I told everyone who was coming to our house to bring their cameras. If Aaron had said that he was in the pictures before, then maybe he would be again. We took pictures all day. Finally, we gathered up the courage to take a look at them on the computer.

We couldn't believe our eyes. In many of the pictures there were white, translucent balls, floating in midair. We found out that they are called orbs. Was that Aaron? In a group family picture that I took a very vivid orb was right above Tom's head. It was so noticeable, not to be missed, just as Aaron would have it. These orbs were very present and very obvious. I had never noticed them in any other picture before. We researched what we could about these things called orbs. This was so amazing. Could this be another miracle? Could we really see proof that he was with us?

I had scheduled another reading with Melanie on Aaron's birthday. I had put two of these pictures with orbs in them into my purse, with the intention of showing them to Melanie at my reading.

Again my reading was just incredible, with more confirmations and validations from Aaron, always expressing his love for us. He mentioned the candle that we lit for him on Thanksgiving, the one in the silver candle stick holder that was in our dining room. He also mentioned that I had placed a picture of him that his Nana had given me next to that candle. He said that he didn't like that picture. How "Aaron"! He brought up the fact that Thanksgiving was one of his favorite holidays, but that he didn't like turkey; it was all about the other food. He knew that I had gone to the cemetery that morning and that I had brought a balloon for him: He said that he had let it go.

During my reading I asked the question of him about the pictures that he had mentioned in his aunt Cheri's reading. Where was he in the pictures and was he in the pictures that we took at Thanksgiving too? While I was posing these questions to Melanie, she began tapping her shoulder with her hand. Over and over she tapped her shoulder and she was saying, "It's on your shoulder. He's on your shoulder."

I asked her if this was from the anniversary party or from Thanksgiving and she said that Aaron told her that it was from Thanksgiving.

Well, I almost fell off my chair! I could barely control myself, wanting to jump up and down. I hadn't even mentioned the pictures that I had brought with me, much less shown them to Melanie. One of the photos was of me on Thanksgiving Day, with a very large, white orb right on my shoulder. Needless to say, I never did take those pictures out of my purse to show Melanie that day. I had the answer that I was really hoping to receive. As we continue to take pictures, even to this day, Aaron is present in a lot of them and almost always if his brother Jeffrey is in the photo as well. It's the first thing that I look for: to see if he's there.

The week after my reading on Aaron's birthday Melanie held a group reading. We had all found out about it at the last minute through my niece, Lindsay. The news spread quickly and many of us wanted to attend: my mom, my sister-in-laws, Aaron's girlfriend and some of our other friends. I couldn't believe how lucky I was to be able to go to see her again, so soon after just meeting with her. I was as excited as I could be, almost more so because now I knew that I truly might hear from Aaron again.

As we all sat with this group of strangers for the event I was simply amazed. Melanie stood at the front of the room, where she delivered many wonderful validations to all of us. It was such an amazing thing to witness not only the incredible validations that my family and friends were receiving, but also to hear validations that complete strangers were receiving and to witness immediately the profound effect that these messages had on them. Many cried tears of joy. Then she said it: "the Bunny." That was all Melanie said, just two simple words: "the Bunny". Then she looked right at Lindsay. The message was from Jennifer, her sister. My brother David, Lindsay and Jennifer's Dad, was not at this event, but we taped it and could not wait to tell him about it. We could hardly control our excitement when we heard those words. Finally, David would hear the words from Jennifer that he had been waiting so long to hear.

It seemed as though I was constantly lost in my own thoughts since Aaron's death. It's odd, but I could carry on conversations with myself all day long in my mind. My brain seemed to never stop working. I had so many questions as I tried to work through this, to make some sense of the madness. I had been trying so hard to figure out how to grasp what had happened, and now, with this new knowledge that Aaron really is here with me, I felt that I could once again, wrap my arms around him too. I kept asking myself, why was I so special that I had received this gift from him? I knew that he had made it possible for me to know that he is here. This lifting of the heart doesn't happen for everyone, or can it? Is it because I refused to give him up? Is it because I was any more deserving than the countless other parents who have lost a child?

The more that I learn, the more that becomes clear to me and the more that becomes a mystery to me. As some things become clearer, I ponder new questions that always present themselves. I now understand that Aaron is here with me, in this different form. I am and will forever be grateful for that. But, if all of these miracles are so easily within our grasp, then why, I ask myself every day, can't he just come home? Why can't he come bouncing in the door and say "Hey Mom, what's up? What's for dinner?"

CHAPTER NINE

Aaron's Angel, Our Christmas Miracle

We have a tradition of celebrating Christmas Eve at our house by building a fire in the woods and cooking hot dogs out under the stars. This is something that we started when the boys were babies. We went outdoors and looked for signs of Santa. It has grown through the years to include family and friends. This tradition is considered by our boys as almost more important and exciting than Christmas Day. It has evolved, however, over the years: everyone migrates into the house for a night of celebrating as soon as the hot dogs and hot cocoa have been devoured.

I wanted so much to keep things as normal as possible for the boys that year, yet nothing was normal. It would be another first without Aaron and no one really knew what to do. What do you do? I wanted to hide, to sleep through all of the holiday events then to wake up when it was all over or maybe not.

Ultimately the boys said that they wanted to continue our traditional celebration, so Christmas Eve was planned. I was dreading all of it and I think that everyone else was feeling the same. But we planned the evening; everyone would come and put on a brave face. Wouldn't you know it; it rained like crazy that Christmas Eve night. It never rains like that on Christmas Eve in Upstate New York. A blizzard of a snow storm is possible, but never a rainstorm. What a blessing that was. The pressure to carry on as usual was off everyone. There would be no outdoor roasting of hot dogs. The gathering took place indoors and we didn't have to struggle through our traditional celebration. I know now for certain that Aaron was looking after us that night too.

Christmas Day arrived. We tried to smile, but our hearts were crying. We opened our gifts with Grandma and Grandpa and sat down at the table for a cup of coffee. Our phone rang. It was the next layer of our Christmas miracle.

I truly can say that I wished that I didn't have to talk to anyone when my phone rang that Christmas Day. I didn't want to wish anyone a Merry Christmas or exchange pleasantries. All I really wanted to do was to scream at the top of my lungs that this was so wrong. Sometimes I chuckle at the irony of it all. I could be going through the motions and look calm and collected, while inside I was screaming and screaming and screaming.

Tom answered the phone that day as we were sitting and drinking coffee with his parents. He said that it was Melanie May calling for me. Melanie? For me? I took the phone and immediately Melanie apologized for calling me on Christmas. She said, though, that she thought that I wouldn't mind the call once she told me the reason for it. She then said that Aaron was with her at that moment and he would not leave her alone, repeatedly telling her to "call my mother, call her now". I couldn't believe what Melanie was saying; I could hardly comprehend it. Was she saying Aaron? My Aaron? With her? Now? I wanted to lock myself in a closet with the phone. "Say it again. Please let me hear those words again". Aaron? Aaron. Little did either of us know, at that moment that this would be only the first demonstration of Aaron's determination. We also didn't realize what an important part of Melanie's life that he would become. Neither of us would have it any other way.

Melanie said that she was having Christmas Brunch with her family and friends when my son Aaron's spirit came to her. He told her that she needed to call me right away and to tell us that he loved us. Melanie was quite familiar by this time with Aaron's spirit, and she recognized him right away. She asked him to patiently wait, as she was with her guests. She told him that she would call me as soon as she could. It was, after all, Christmas. Well, holiday or no holiday Aaron wasn't having any of that. He continued to pressure Melanie: she began to shake. As I later learned from her, she will sometimes start to shake when a spirit is very strong and wants her attention. Some of her girlfriends were sitting with her that morning and saw what was happening to her. They knew right away that a spirit was trying to contact her.

Melanie explained to them who Aaron was, but said that she was uncomfortable calling me on Christmas Day and intruding on my holiday. Are you kidding? Thank goodness her friends realized that it would be the ultimate present for any mother to hear from her son on Christmas. Melanie agreed, excused herself because Aaron wouldn't wait, and made the call to me. She said that Aaron had been with Tom and me that morning at the cemetery and was with us now. He said that he loved us.

Believe me, if I could have squeezed this full-grown body through that tiny little phone wire all the way to her end and given her the biggest hug, I would have. To say the least this had been such a hard, sad day for all of us. Now Melanie was delivering this message, this miracle from our son.

Aaron also told Melanie that I had just received an angel for a gift. He said to tell me about the angel so that I would trust that this message was real. I couldn't believe what she was saying. Not ten minutes before her call I had opened a gift from Tom's parents. It was indeed an angel. I told Melanie, that yes I did just receive an angel.

Melanie said, "I know, Aaron is telling me that it is small, bronze metal, flat and has a little sparkle to it". It was described in perfect detail. "OH MY GOD", was all that I could say over and over. We talked a little more. During the conversation I just wanted to ask her more, to beg her not to hang up. I was so grateful for this message that it was almost too hard to speak. Before we did hang up, however, Melanie mentioned that the appointment planner for her business had been stolen from her car on Christmas Eve. Since so many of Aaron's family and friends now went to see her, she asked me to relay a message to anyone who might have an appointment with her. She asked that they call her with the time and date that they were scheduled. How awful, I thought, that someone would do such a thing. Melanie helps so many people. She didn't deserve to be robbed. No one does, especially not her.

After I hung up from our conversation, I relayed the messages from Aaron to Tom and his parents. We cried, yet our hearts soared at this powerful affirmation from our son. If anyone could accomplish something like this, Aaron could. He would find a way to ease our pain. No matter what he had to do, he would do it. We told everyone that we could about this amazing miracle. We talked about how these events reminded Tom of the movie Ghost, with the actress Whoopie Goldberg. By the way, did I mention that many of the pictures taken on that Christmas Day also contained our beloved orbs in them? Of course they did.

This euphoria, for which I should be so grateful, did not last long. By Christmas night I was taking down the tree. I was so thankful for how the day had turned out. Never, not even in my wildest dreams, did I expect to hear such news. It still didn't change the fact, however, that Aaron wasn't here, that things weren't the way they used to be, the way they should be. I simply wanted the holiday to be over and done with.

The day after Christmas started as any other. I would try to get through the whole "holiday thing" with a smile on my face. I was upstairs getting dressed and I couldn't keep my mind from returning to yesterday's sequence of events. I wanted to pinch myself, to make sure that I wasn't dreaming it all. Did I truly grasp what had happened, the magnitude of what my son was doing to reassure us that he was okay? What had started out to be one of my most dreaded days was now forever etched in my heart as a gift beyond measure. I was thinking, as I got dressed, just how much I missed Aaron. I also knew that he would never have stood by and let someone steal something as important as her work planner from Melanie. Aaron had always seemed to be the man of the hour if someone needed a little help. I knew that he would be taking care of everything, if only he were here and knew that this had been stolen from her. I just knew that he really would have been enraged, especially after all that she had done for him and his family.

As I came downstairs that morning my phone was ringing. I answered the call: it was a sobbing Melanie. I could barely understand what she was saying. My heart started pounding. What was wrong? Why was she crying? Why was she calling me again? I had no idea what this call was going to be about, but I knew in that instant that I was so glad that she was calling me. Whatever the reason, I knew that I was so grateful to be on the other end of her call.

Melanie was crying and trying to talk. All I could make out was "Aaron"! Finally, after many aborted attempts and unrecognizable words, she calmed herself down and started to explain what had happened. Aaron, she said, had come to her in a dream the night before. He had picked her up and she floated above her bed, safe and secure with him. She was surrounded in pure love. As they looked down, she saw herself with her husband as he was handing her a Christmas gift. She watched herself open the box, reach inside, and then give the empty box to him. Her husband said to her, "Wait there is something else still in the box." Melanie reached back inside and took out a small flat box that she opened. Inside was a beautiful angel. Melanie said that it was the same angel that I had received the day before, on Christmas. Aaron told Melanie that this angel was a gift from him to her to thank her for all that she had done to help his family. He also told her that he would help her, that he would get her planner for her.

In the morning, when Melanie woke up from her dream visit with Aaron, she told everyone in her house that she was going to get her planner back. She said that she knew without a doubt that this would happen and she was so happy. Her mother and family who were visiting for the holidays asked her what she was talking about and she told them that Aaron had told her that he would help her. She was elated and so sure that that same day, this gesture of gratitude from Aaron and miracle of love would unfold. Melanie was just sitting down to send an e-mail to me to explain this magnificent dream visit that she had had from my son. As she was actually typing the letter "A" to begin spelling "Aaron", her phone rang. Melanie said that she started screaming and ran to answer the phone. "My planner, that's about my planner. They're calling to say that they've found my planner!!!!" Sure enough, it was a salesperson from the furniture store in her town calling to say that a planner, belonging to Melanie May, had been turned in to them. Melanie said that although she had been convinced by the previous night' dream that this event would take place. She was nonetheless completely overwhelmed by it all.

The abilities and laws of the spirit world are still quite a mystery to us, even to Melanie who deals with their world each day. Aaron's gratitude and sincere love left her with no doubts that he would fulfill his promise. Over the past several months she had been given an introduction to Aaron's presence and I was hoping and praying that it would turn into a very long-lasting relationship.

In the midst of all of the happiness and reliving of the sequence of events, Melanie's husband went to retrieve her planner. The people at the store said only that a young man found it and said that it needed to be returned to the owner. He never left his name or any other information. The name of the store where the planner had been turned in was Goldbergs. Another coincidence? My husband had used the exact name when trying to make an analogy of the previous day's events for his parents. He had recounted the story of the movie Ghost to his parents and the role of the actress, Whoopie Goldberg.

How could so many miraculous events have taken place as they had over the previous months without the hand of some divine intervention? These things are not commonplace, or are they? Are events and subtleties much more common than we think and only waiting to be noticed?

The more that I learn, the more that I gratefully experience, the more that I don't know. To be open to receiving these wonderful gifts means letting go of your fears and expectations. When you think that's all that you have left, it's not so easy to do.

Chapter Ten

Out of Something Bad Comes Something Good

My relationship with Melanie has grown into a beautiful friendship. We seemed to have an instant connection, as if we had always known each other. Now I work for Melanie. This, too, was made possible with the help of Aaron.

I didn't know that prior to our Christmas miracle Melanie had been contemplating, with great apprehension, the need for someone to help her with her business. This was not something that she was in a hurry to do. Her business is very important to her and the thought of relinquishing some of the control of it scared her.

I was just barely able to put one foot in front of the other, and definitely not looking for any kind of job. Aaron had different ideas.

While Melanie was talking to me on the day after Christmas, in the midst of all my wonder and gratitude, Aaron told Melanie to "ask my mother to work for you".

Despite having no previous intention of doing so, Melanie asked me if I would be interested in handling her phone calls and scheduling appointments for readings. I know that at that time I was having trouble making any decisions at all and surely would have refused such an offer. However, that is not what sprang from my lips. I told her that of course, I would love to work for her and I meant it. To be involved daily in this new, interesting world was exactly what I wanted and needed to do. I wanted to learn everything that I could about the spirit world and the afterlife. I wanted so strongly to keep my connection with my son alive and well. Neither one of us had expected this to happen, but Aaron assured us that it was exactly what we both needed.

Without hesitation I accepted her offer. We worked out the particulars and before I knew it, it was my voice answering the phone in the office of Melanie May.

I've heard the saying many times that "Out of something bad comes something good". I used to think that whoever said that didn't know my grief. Now, as I go through each day, I am beginning to understand.

I have to honestly say that I am so thankful to be able to work with Melanie and to have her as such a dear friend. I find my role so very healing and uplifting for me. Little did I know that by being on the other end of this lifeline of a phone call, I would be helped to come back to the living; just a little more each day. As the calls came into her office from people all over the country who wanted so badly to connect with someone whom they had lost, I began to understand.

Those calls were pulling me out of my self-absorbed life of grief, perhaps for only a few minutes at a time, but I saw that this terrible feeling that I had was so commonplace. Every day, every minute, someone else was being thrown into the sorrowful existence that I was living, and I started to realize that I could play a small role in lessening their pain.
As I talked with the strangers who called, I began to find myself listening to those who wanted to tell me their story. I sometimes offered a few words describing my own experience to help ease the uncertainty and apprehension for some.

So many times the callers would offer only minimal information on their part, so any chance of the medium (Melanie) researching information about them prior to their scheduled meetings would be eliminated. I could definitely identify with their concerns; it's exactly how I felt when I scheduled my first appointment. I didn't want Melanie to know any information at all about me. If only they knew that is the last thing Melanie would do.

It doesn't work that way. The information that she gets from the spirits is always information that will validate to you that they are there. If information is known beforehand, then that is not what your loved ones will bring to you. The validations are very often something that you would never expect or imagine, but are true. Many times these validations are about very recent events, even as recent as the conversations that you may have had in the car on your way to your appointment. The validations are significant only in that they establish that the information is truly from a loved one.

It is amazing, and I hear about these miracles each and every day. Just when I think that this really can't be happening to me, when I think that I can't go on another day without Aaron, I witness another miracle and I am assured again that he truly is here with me still. It's as if he keeps pinching me every now and then to let me know that he is here.

CHAPTER ELEVEN

Angels Do Exist Among Us

Sometimes someone will come into your life and you're not sure exactly why they did, but you know in that first instant when you meet them that you're so glad that they did. They simply show up, or send you a message or call you just when you are in need of it most.

How do they do that? That's how I define a true friend. To me it's the definition of an angel. Some of these people you see often; others you see less frequently, but time has no effect on the relationship. You pick up right where you left off, without skipping a beat. We all have these angels in our lives; at least I hope that we all do. I know that I am blessed with many such friends and I am so grateful for each one. I also hope that I am that kind of friend in someone else's life.

When our nightmare first began, one of my friends gave me a journal and told me to write what was in my heart. I never imagined that I could write anything but ugly, agonizing words. Write to whom? Certainly she couldn't mean to Aaron. Write about this terrible tragedy? I had nothing to say; I had only questions. Then, when I least expected to hear it again, another friend had the same suggestion. We were talking about the mailbox that my brother had put at Aaron's grave. She too told me, that I should write and that she had the perfect title, Aaron's Mailbox.

Although I had no intention of writing I just couldn't resist agreeing with her and her great big heart. Her genuine warmth reminds me so much of Aaron.   Perhaps her destiny was to help me fill that void created by his absence. I didn't use the journal at first, but as the year progressed, I kept thinking of writing everything down. I wanted to capture all of the miracles as they happened, to record each and every one. I thought about the mailbox at Aaron's grave, but never thought that I could deal with expressing my own emotions. As I put down these words however, it has suddenly made sense to use the suggested title of this book. I thought that I couldn't possibly write down my innermost thoughts and feelings to him.

I thought that I could never get through my own tears. I want no part of being able to merely honor Aaron's memory or to admit that something good always comes from something bad.

If I did those things, then I would have to admit that this whole thing is real. Aaron really isn't coming home.

I think that if I stay in the moment, the moments when he is communicating with us, then that's all I need. That can be my reality, the only reality. As I look back at these written words of pain and fear and love, I realize that he is showing me just one more unimaginable miracle.

I know that I am somehow supposed to be able to let go of him now because I know in my heart that he is with me always.

Until this very moment, I have never been able to even think those words. But as I write them down now, difficult as it is, I do know that I need only to reach down deep into my heart, and he's right here.

CHAPTER TWELVE

They Are Champions

From the first moment that I met Melanie May I have been so blessed to have many, many amazing messages of love, compliments of my son Aaron. As Melanie would relay messages almost daily, and surely when I needed them the most, I couldn't believe how each one was so amazing and accurate.

Although I couldn't comprehend any of what was taking place at the 2008 Final Four and Championship Lacrosse games, we did have the games on television and many people were at our house to cheer on our boys. I have been told many times over that the game between Syracuse and Virginia was a miracle in itself: the way in which it played out and how Syracuse came back to win. Oh, really? According to recounts from my sons Kyle and Thomas, as well as the other players, there was no doubt on their part that they would win that game. A loss was unthinkable. So, of course they won against all odds, and proceeded to clinch the national title in the next game as well. I know that Kyle has said that he asked his brother Aaron to help him get through those games, and Aaron has since taken some credit for doing so.

When the next year's season came around, lacrosse was the last thing I wanted to think about. Kyle had graduated, but Thomas was still at Syracuse and needed our support. Each game day was eagerly awaited by the team, parents and fans, but for me each game day was a benchmark of how many days we would have had left with Aaron. I would think back to the previous year not knowing then that the remaining days that we would have him with us were few. As everyone cheered on the team, I was constantly reliving the previous year, holding back tears and counting the days. When the team made it to the Final Four again, I was devastated inside.

How could I possibly get through the upcoming anniversary of Aaron's death, and at the same time be supportive and cheer on my son Thomas? The last place on earth that I ever wanted to see was that stadium. I know that it was so selfish, but why did they have to make it to the finals this year? Couldn't we just wait and let some other team have a turn? Why us again? As hard as it was to say so to Thomas, I just couldn't make myself go to those games.

I chose instead to go to Toronto to watch our son Kyle, who was playing on a professional lacrosse team. While my husband Tom and son Jeffrey went to Boston to cheer on Thomas, I went to Kyle's game on Friday in Toronto.

I returned home on Saturday, in time for the second half of the Syracuse game. I knew that I would learn of the outcome, so I decided to distract myself and go cut the lawn.

I was mowing and having one big pity party for myself: I was fed up with life, crying about how unfair this was, and missing Aaron so badly.

When I came inside the house the phone rang. Reluctantly, I answered it and Melanie was on the other end. "Aaron said to "KNOCK IT OFF, MA"!!!" That's my boy; ya gotta love him! Now, I was smiling through all of those tears.

Syracuse won that game on Saturday. They were off to the championship round again, on Monday. Well, self-pity or no self-pity, I had to go for Thomas' sake. How could I take it out on him, deny him because of my pain? Aaron definitely was not going to quietly stand by and let me stay home and sulk. So, off I went to Boston and to the men's lacrosse national championship game.

The championship game was three quarters of the way done and it wasn't looking very good for Syracuse. We were playing Cornell and it looked as if they would be the next champions. Cornell was playing at the top of their game and Syracuse just couldn't seem to catch a break. The stadium was roaring, as all of the Cornell fans were going crazy with celebration, sure that they would win. I don't know how, but suddenly, through all that noise, I heard my cell phone ring. I answered the call and it was Melanie.

"We're going to score; we are going to win. Aaron said that we are going to win !!!!" She said.

It's a good thing that I had grown pretty comfortable with having Aaron send me messages when I least expected them. A victory by SU seemed highly unlikely, but I knew in that moment that there was nothing to worry about. Syracuse was down, with only seconds left in the game. It would take a miracle to pull off a win. Did I say miracle?

Cornell had the ball and it definitely looked as though they would have the victory. I yelled to Tom, who was in the seat next to me, "We're going to score; we are going to win the game. Aaron said so."

Tom just looked at me with a yeah, okay, now-I-know-that-you-have-lost-it look, and he continued to watch the game. Within a split second, Syracuse somehow got the ball back and scored, tying the game up and sending it into overtime. Both teams had opportunities to win in sudden victory. Each team had won turns at controlling the ball, but was denied scoring. Syracuse suddenly had the ball, shot it, and into the net it went. It was complete chaos. How on earth could that possibly have happened? The noise was deafening with screams and celebrations.

"I told you that they would win", I said to Tom.

When I later spoke with Melanie, she told me that she had been at a party watching the game, when Aaron told her that we were going to win. She started shouting to everyone there that Syracuse would win. A policeman friend of hers, knowing very well that it was close to impossible said, "yeah, sure". When the goal was made and Syracuse had won the game, the man turned to Melanie and asked, "How do you do that?" Melanie only said, "You have to know Aaron"!

CHAPTER THIRTEEN

There Is No Time In Heaven

Have you ever sat and wondered just how far back in time events in your life were set into motion in order for them to unfold as they do? For each minute, each second of your life, what had to happen in the past to have the present unfold as it does? These are serious, deep thought-provoking questions. If you think about it, and seriously ask yourself that question, your mind can take you places so far away that you feel as though you have been lost in the abyss.

With my new knowledge of our existence after we die, it seems to me that I am always thinking of new questions. The materials and books that I have read, the conversations that I have had, the spiritual people that I have listened to, all say the same thing. There is no time as we know it on the other side. How we measure things- the past, the present, the future- does not exist in the spirit world. Every moment is now.

Well, I would really like to read the rule book or the manual that explains all of this, because this concept is really reaching far beyond the limits of my thinking power. I find that if I just touch upon the surface of this topic and don't try to dig too deeply, then I can digest some of its meaning. The moment I try to contemplate and comprehend this idea of no time, I end up only adding to my very long list of questions that most likely will not be answered for me during my lifetime.

This concept of time being a measurement only in this physical life must be an important factor in gaining a further understanding of the spiritual life. I would like to share with you a very profound example of how this theory has been proven to me.

For many years we had a clock hanging on the wall in our kitchen. I thought it was an interesting clock and it could be set to open up and play a tune at intervals of the hour. It was a more modern version of a cuckoo clock. As you walked into our kitchen the clock was right in front of you and it was what you saw as you entered. My sons did not like this clock; Aaron especially would voice his opinion about it. "That clock is really lame, Mom. Don't turn on the sound; just leave it." My mom had given us the clock, so I really felt that I should hang it up and that the kitchen was the best location.

Well, sometime after Aaron's accident we realized that the clock had stopped keeping time. I replaced the batteries several times but the clock would not work. Although this had occurred shortly after Aaron's accident, I felt no urgency to do anything with the clock. I just left it on the wall, aware that it was not working despite my attempts with new batteries. I just left it alone.

It was months later, long after I had met Melanie and started receiving Aaron's wonderful messages, that he had her call me with another one. "I don't know how to tell you this without offending you, so I'm just going to say it because he is telling me to do so. Aaron says that he really does not like the clock that you have hanging on the wall."

I laughed and told her the story of how he really didn't like that clock. It registered in that moment why the clock had stopped working when it did and why new batteries had no effect.

Okay, I'm listening.

I took the clock down as soon as we finished our phone conversation and that place where it had hung stayed empty for quite a while. Everyone who came into the house would ask what had happened to the clock.

The next winter Tom and I decided to do some remodeling on our kitchen. Things were definitely starting to look worse for the wear after twenty-five years so we decided to delve into a project to keep our minds and hands busy.

Since the blue heron had become such a significant sign of Aaron to me, I had decided that it would be here in the kitchen that I would display the pictures of herons that we had taken, as well as the heron statues that I had found. It would be so fitting to have the room where I spend most of my time focused on something that makes me think of Aaron.

I was showing my Mom the pictures of the herons that I had and she said, "You know, I think that the picture that I have hanging in my hall that Aaron made for me years ago is a heron". No way! I knew the picture that she was talking about: it was hanging in her hallway where she displayed all of the artwork that her grandchildren had made for her when they were younger. I had seen the picture a million times, but had never made the connection. Are you sure? A heron? So I went and got it from her house. I couldn't believe what I saw as I looked at the picture through much different eyes. It was made by an eleven year old Aaron when he was in school in 1998, exactly ten years before his death. It was a picture that he had made in art class: you color the entire sheet of paper with black and then scrape the black off to reveal the whiteness underneath in your desired image. It had his name in big block letters in the top left corner, with the date and the letters SU underneath. It was definitely a heron.

My mind wanted to explode and I was whirling with questions. Did he know? Did he have some inner awareness that his life would be so short? Did he know that it would be the heron that he would send to me as a special sign from him? Did he know way back then, when he was just a little boy, that the terrible tragedy of his death would occur and that he would need to leave behind something for me to be able to touch and feel?

I was spinning with emotions. Finding this picture made me smile and it made me cry. Why? Just how far back in time were these events, any events, put into motion? Where does it all begin and will it end? Could I have changed one small act and would our lives have had a different outcome?

Aaron had left nothing to chance. He had cleared the way to find just the perfect spot for his heron picture. Almost everyone who comes to our house knows that Aaron has sent the blue heron to us as a sign. I have told this to all of our family and friends, but no one knew about his drawing of the heron. Now, as they step into our kitchen, they usually just stop in their tracks, as their eyes take in Aaron's picture which hangs where the "lame" clock used to hang.

Sometimes..... there are no words.

PART II

CHAPTER FOURTEEN

Life Now, With Aaron

How do I begin this next chapter in my life? Everything that we knew had been completely changed. That horrible night in May, 2008 changed everything so completely; nothing would ever be the same again. I look back now, with a clearer head and knowledge of the spirit world and its co-existence with our world, and I realize that Aaron was trying to tell me immediately, right after his accident, that he would find a way to get through to me. He sent messages, placed objects in our paths, circulated fragrances that smelled just like him; he did anything that he could do to assure us that he wasn't far away.

The year following Aaron's death is so very hard to explain, to say the least. It was sometimes a violent roller-coaster ride with emotional twists and turns everywhere I looked. Sometimes I would begin to think that I could understand some of this, only to go crashing down without any warning. I knew that I just needed a year to sit and think, to do nothing else; to just think it through. I do know now that it wasn't my own mind chatter working overtime. It was Aaron getting through to me right from the beginning, I just didn't recognize that fact at the time, and it took me just about a year for it all to connect.

I have been blessed to have a wonderful son, who in spirit frequently insists on getting his message through to me, and a wonderful friend to relay those messages. I have thought long and hard about Melanie's gift of intuition, and I can't help wonder: if she can do it, why can't I, or anyone else for that matter? Of course, I know that her abilities are definitely exceptional, but maybe all of us could become somewhat connected, if we really wanted to. Well, I wanted nothing more and I set myself on a path to see what might unfold, privately determined to make it happen.

Just when I think that I can't possibly go on another day, not another minute, Aaron seems to show up. He always seems to know when I need him most and sends some sort of message for me so that I can take a few steps and then a few more. Once, wasn't going to be good enough for me, though. Each time that I would receive a life-saving validation from Aaron, I would be elated, but the euphoria wouldn't last long and I would find myself slipping back down into my world of grief all too soon. Aaron obviously knows me better than I know myself and he is always there, reassuring and confirming that he is with me.

Since my introduction to Melanie, he has continued to send messages through her, and some directly through to me. As each message is delivered I scurry to write it down, so that I will never forget. My journal book is not neatly written pages. It's filled with sticky notes and scraps of paper that were handy at the moment so that I could write down each word.

CHAPTER FIFTEEN

Messages Sent With Love From Aaron

As we learned about Melanie May and her amazing gifts, we were so absorbed in the miraculous and life-changing effect that her gift had for all of us that we never really stopped to notice the effect that Aaron was having on Melanie. We were so overjoyed with each new bit of information or validation from him and we couldn't wait to hear what would come next.

Our Christmas miracle from Aaron was definitely more than any of us could have hoped for. Not in our wildest dreams did we ever hope to receive for such signs of grace and love from our son.

The Christmas angel and miracle events had quite an effect on Melanie as well. She was beginning to realize that Aaron was very insistent on getting his messages to us. Time and time again, he let Melanie know in a loving manner, of course, just who was really in charge. When she tried to hold him off, her body began to shake. Many times after that morning, Aaron would ask Melanie to relay a message and if for some reason she would delay his request, even for the briefest time, he would quickly insist "Call my mother now".

I was grateful beyond words for the messages that Melanie brought to me from my son, and just as grateful for the wonderful friendship with her that seemed to develop so quickly. It didn't take long before we were talking several times a day, sometimes about business, but mostly as friends. I think that this was another reason why Aaron was so insistent that our paths should cross.

Aaron also became very watchful over Melanie. She told me many times that he was so clear and articulate when communicating with her, and she called upon him often to help her or to guide her.

On Monday evenings Melanie would travel to the homes of clients, where she would do readings for small groups. These gatherings were always very draining on her, physically and emotionally. Part of my role that seemed to quickly evolve was to talk to Melanie as she drove to and from these gatherings. She would call me and we would chat; this would help her stay focused and alert on the drive. As this routine developed, it became apparent that Aaron would also be along for the ride. As soon as Melanie would get into the car, he would make himself known. A couple of times she started her car, put it into drive, and he would tell her "Wait. You forgot to turn your lights on". Many times we would be talking and Melanie would make a wrong turn and get herself completely lost. She would always say to me, "Hold on while I ask Aaron how to get back to where I need to go". Within seconds, she would tell me what she needed to do and be on the correct path again.

After my first reading with Melanie I wanted so badly for Tom and the boys to experience what I had, so I asked her to come to our house to do a reading for them. This was before our Christmas angel miracle and before I began working for Melanie so they did not know her at all. I wanted them to feel comfortable in their own home, knowing full well that they would never go to her office. This was way too far out of their comfort zone.

Aaron helped Melanie find us. It was a Monday evening and when she got to our house the first thing that she said to me was that Aaron had helped her find her way here. She had used her GPS to guide her with directions to our house. We live on country roads so there are not many landmarks other than road signs. Melanie said that when she came to intersecting roads a few streets from our house, the GPS said that she had reached her destination. Well, she knew that she hadn't because she was sitting at a street corner, with not a house in sight and it was pitch dark. She had forgotten her phone, so she was starting to panic. She thought about turning around, backtracking a bit and starting again. Just as she was about to turn the car, Aaron said to her, "I will show you how to get to my house. I'll take you there." He then proceeded to direct her right to our door. She said that she had no doubt and just followed his directions.

Aaron continued to watch over her and protect her each and every Monday evening. One time, we were talking as she drove her weekly trip and she said that Aaron was with her in the car. Since it was wintertime and I knew that the roads could be tricky, I said "Don't worry, Aaron will keep you safe." Melanie said that he had just said those same words to her too.

The weather was turning worse and it was beginning to snow very hard, so we decided to hang up so that Melanie could concentrate on driving. She called me just a short time later to say that just as we had finished talking, she could actually feel Aaron press down on her brakes and slow her car. He said "slow down, slow down". As the car slowed, she rounded a corner. There, in the blinding snow in front of her, was a man crossing the road. Surely she would not have been able to avoid hitting him if she were going any faster. Melanie has told me on several occasions that Aaron has slowed her car down physically or told her to slow down. The reason always became quickly clear.

As Melanie and I were soon to find out, Aaron was there often in both our lives. He always seemed to send a message when I needed one the most. Even though Melanie lived this life each day, communicating with our loved ones, she found that she herself was learning and growing with Aaron right by her side. She described Aaron's role as it was emerging in her life: he was her gatekeeper, always there to guide and protect her. He would not let anything bad happen to her.

You would think that perhaps this information would make me sad or leave me asking "why not for me"? The opposite is true. I always knew that Aaron would take care of everyone. He was always that type of person and it is one of the most confirming validations for me.

 Melanie called to say that she was doing laundry, and Aaron asked her to call me and tell me that he loved me. He said to tell me that he had been with me in the car as I drove home from her house the day before. She then told me that as she was watching a movie with her family Aaron told her to check her e-mail, that his Mom had just sent her an e-mail. Sure enough, at that moment, I had just hit the send button.

 Tom and I had just gotten back from the store. The phone rang as we entered the house. It was Melanie and she said that her message was for Tom. She had just remembered a dream that she had only a night or two before. In the dream Aaron told her that something had happened with his shoes or his boots over the past week. Tom replied that he had started wearing Aaron's boots to work the previous week. Aaron said that he was happy that Tom was wearing his boots.

Melanie said that Aaron was telling her that Junior; his girlfriend's three year old brother, was bouncing up and down, just bouncing up and down. I called Malinda, Aaron's girlfriend. She said that Junior was bouncing up and down with his cousin as we were speaking. The next week Junior came to my house. He was bouncing up and down as he was talking to me, exactly as Aaron used to do when he was a young boy.

Melanie reported that as I was leaving her home- just pulling out of the driveway- Aaron said to her "Road Runner, beep beep." What did that mean? I had cleaned out the desk the day before and thrown out a box with the Road Runner character on it.

Aaron told Melanie again that he was happy that his Dad was wearing his boots!

I received an e-mail from Melanie that asked "Did something just happen with the toaster? Did it break or something?" I e-mailed back to ask her, asking whether it could be "poster" that he was saying? When she opened the email, she knew immediately that yes, it was "poster". She does not get the audio part of intuition as clearly as the feeling. "As soon as I read your message Aaron hit me with confirmation energy. He was with you all morning!"

Later that day Melanie called me. She said that Aaron was there with her again and that he was so strong when he came through that she wished that she could bottle "that energy" to show me. Aaron told her that he saw me hanging up a photograph poster with the boys' pictures on it. I was hanging up actual posters of the 2008 lacrosse championship team; Thomas and Kyle were in the photos. He also mentioned the bird on the little wooden thing that hangs. That week Tom's sister, Mary, had given Tom and me each a wooden disc which hangs as an ornament. It had a heron etched on it. I had put mine by the kitchen sink so that I could see it. The blue heron has come many times during December, even with all the snow. We took pictures of it.

 Melanie called me on her weekly Monday night ride home. She said that she had this tall, handsome guy riding with her and that he wanted her to call me and say "Road Runner" to me again. How funny, I had been thinking about the Road Runner thing that day and read what I had written about it in my journal. She said that the weather was bad as she was driving, but Aaron would keep her safe. He told her that he would stay with her as she was driving. He also told her that he loved to eat ice cream. That was very true. Ice cream was one of his very favorite foods and he could eat the entire half gallon of ice cream at one sitting; if he let himself.

The next morning I turned on the TV at 7:20am and what was on, but a commercial for Road Runner internet service. Of course!

 During a reading that Melanie was giving Aaron had a message for Melanie's client. He wanted to thank her for starting the chain. This client had told Laura about Melanie, and Laura had told me. Only Aaron knew that this chain of events had occurred. Neither Melanie, nor the client had any idea of how the connections had been made; I didn't either. Now we all know.

 I am trying to be more observant of the signs that are happening for me. I was driving on the highway and thought that I should call ahead. I had just dialed the number and the first ring sounded, then the phone clicked off. I decided that I should put the phone away while driving and make the call when it was safer to do so. I considered the fact that my phone turned off without any apparent reason, a sign to pay more attention to my driving because it was cold and snowy. A short distance further on I came upon a car accident on the highway going in the other direction. The road conditions were more hazardous than I had first thought. Did Aaron turn off my phone? Are the thoughts that come into your head, your own?

 Malinda, Aaron's girlfriend, was in bed and had started to cry. She said that she felt Aaron touch her shoulder. She immediately fell asleep, and didn't remember the incident until late the next day.

 I was upstairs getting dressed when the thought suddenly occurred to me that I needed to get an angel, like the one from my Christmas miracle, for Melanie. I came down stairs and discovered that it was her birthday that day. Aaron had done it again.

 I found myself thinking about Richmond, Virginia. I didn't know why, as we have no connection to that city. Of course I thought that Aaron must be responsible for these thoughts. Later that day Jeffrey and Tom got back from ice fishing. I asked them if Ben, Aaron's friend, had gone too. Tom said, no, that Ben was in Virginia.

 Melanie said that Aaron wanted her to tell me that he was hugging me back. That morning I had hugged his sweatshirt and told him that I was hugging him. She asked me if I had on a purple shirt or sweater. We were speaking on the phone; she could not see me. I said that yes, I was wearing a purple shirt and a purple sweater. Melanie said that Aaron told her what I was wearing so that I would trust that he really was hugging me in return.

Malinda brought her three year old brother Junior over to visit. He said that the previous day "Guy" – his name for Aaron, told him that he had been eating cookies and milk, sleeping and watching TV. Junior also said that Guy reads his book with him. The book is about barnyard animals and Junior read it aloud with Aaron when they were together on the couch. Junior laughs out loud when he plays by himself as though someone is with him. When his mother asks him what is making him laugh, he says "It's Guy, Mommy, he's tickling me. Can't you see him?"

Melanie called shortly afterward and asked me if we were just talking about Aaron. I said that yes, we were. He told her to say the word "microwave" to me. I would know what he meant and that would help me to trust that the message was really coming from him. Tom and I had been talking the night before about the microwave that we were using in our kitchen. It was the one that we had bought for Aaron to use when he was in school.

 Melanie called me in the morning and said that Aaron was telling her to call his Mom. He told her that I was wearing a blue and white bathrobe as we spoke and that I was holding a yellow coffee cup. This was true. She asked me if my phone had rung in the middle of the night. I said that I didn't think so, that I hadn't heard it ring. Melanie said that Aaron had been trying to call our house the night before. He had shown her this in her dream. She said that she could see him actually trying to push the numbers down. No, I had not heard our phone ring during the night. Later that morning I was on another call. Just as I finished with that call, my phone immediately rang again. It rang only one time and there was no caller ID or message that said incoming call. I knew that it was Aaron calling; I just knew for certain in my heart.

PRØWL™

I called Tom to tell him what had happened. I was so excited I could hardly control myself. As I finished my conversation with Tom, my cell phone rang and this time it was Melanie. As I answered the call, she blurted out "That was him. That was Aaron on the house phone calling you. You knew it was him and he wanted me to call you to tell you that you were right. You knew!" I was beside myself all day. I finally knew that somehow I had him back.

 Melanie is holding a group reading tonight. It is the first one since I have started working for her and I am very excited. Melanie is nervous since this one is quite full, with a lot of Aaron's friends and family present. As she prepares herself before the event, Aaron is with her and tells her that he will help her to get through it. He helps to calm her nerves. As soon as he says this, she is calm and ready to go. Aaron is the first to show up for the group with a "hello" to all of us. He congratulates his aunt who had just quit smoking, and berates his Nana for smoking too much. He tells me that I will write a book. My brother was praying silently then for his daughter Jennifer to bring a message for him. Just then Melanie tells him, "You were scuba diving and you saw something shimmer and sparkle". David had just gotten back from a trip to the tropics and had been scuba diving. He told me of an incident when he saw this most beautiful shimmer and sparkling while diving at night. He said that he was not afraid at all, but knew that Jennifer was there in that sparkle. Well, I guess that he was right. I just love it!

Tom was planning to go ice fishing with Malinda's father, Bob. He had gotten up early and was getting his clothes on and gathering his gear. His cell phone rang; it was 6 a.m. It was Melanie calling him. Aaron woke her up and told her to call his Dad on his cell phone, not the house phone. Aaron told Melanie Tom's cell phone number which at the time she did not know. When Tom answered, Melanie asked him if he was going fishing. This was not something that Tom did often, so Melanie had no prior knowledge of his plans. Tom said that yes, he was just getting ready to leave. Melanie said to him "Aaron says don't go. Don't go ice fishing today." Bob was already on his way over to pick up Tom. When he got to our house, Tom told him what had happened. They both decided to listen to Aaron's advice. I'm not sure what is more miraculous- these amazing messages sent from our son or the fact that all of us now know and trust that they truly are from him.

 This new existence and way of life for us was overwhelming at times. However, I was completely dedicated to embracing any form of communication that I could have with Aaron. I looked forward enthusiastically to the day when I could communicate with him myself. If Melanie could do it, then why couldn't I? I knew that her gift was special, but I thought that surely if I tried hard enough, I could have a little of that too. I read everything that I could on the subject. I listened to guided meditation tapes. I practiced and practiced, trying to ignite some sort of knowingness. If it happened once; when Aaron called our phone and I knew it was him- then hopefully it could happen again. Somehow, someday, I would be able to know without a doubt that he was right there with me at that moment and maybe even know what he was saying to me too. One thing I did know for certain: I would never stop trying. I could do this; I had to do this.

Tom and I were sitting in the sunroom the afternoon that he was supposed to go ice fishing but didn't because of Aaron's warning. We were just so grateful for all of the messages from Aaron. For me it was sometimes paralyzing. All this information made my mind reel, as each new experience made me think of more and more unanswered questions. We discussed the idea that we were unlikely candidates for such miracles. Who could have imagined these things happening to us? My total willingness and drive to embrace all of this was not exactly matched by Tom, but Aaron was pushing harder than ever to let his Dad know that he was there for him.

As we sat there, Tom was on the couch and I was in the office chair. Suddenly I felt this very pronounced sensation on the back of my head, as though a flat top was spinning and spinning. At the same time I knew "Jennifer" (my niece). What was that? Who said that? I said to Tom, "Jennifer's here." He gave me a very strange look and asked "What did you say?"

I said that I didn't know how I knew, but I did know that she was there. The spinning and tingling sensation on the back of my head continued. Wow; "That was really weird," I thought, "but bring it on!"

We continued to sit and talk, but the spiritual moment that I had was brief and finished as quickly as it started. I found it difficult to concentrate on my conversation with Tom. My mind was trying to decipher what had just happened.

A few minutes later I felt a heavy plop on the top of my head; the sensation then started to very slowly ease down my head toward my forehead. This arrival was much more pronounced than the feeling on the back of my head and I thought of a big bird or airplane skidding in for landing without much grace. Boom! And in an instant my mind "knew". Aaron! Oh my God! YES!!!!

This is what I wanted more than anything. I knew that he was there. Once I regained my composure and logically thought about it, it made perfect sense that Aaron would make his presence known in this manner to me. The feeling reminded me of the many times I had seen a duck land on our pond. It would seem to fall down from the sky and plop into the water. No stealth skills were utilized; just a great big splash was produced to announce his arrival. As if to say "here I am". That was Aaron's style as well- to make a grand entrance- and duck hunting on the water was one of his favorite things to do. I wanted to scream and jump up and down, but I was afraid to move my head for fear he would go away.

I said to Tom "AARON"S HERE, I can feel AARON!" Well, now he was really looking at me as though I had gone over the edge. I couldn't believe it. I couldn't explain it. I couldn't prove it. But I knew it.

February 10, 2009. Melanie calls to say that Aaron was there with her. He told her that sometime in the future I would tell her about something that happens to me. He wanted her to write a description of the future event down and date it, so that when it happened, she could show the paper to me.

A month or so after that conversation, I was shopping with my sister-in law. We came upon two ornamental blue herons in the store. I couldn't believe it. I had never seen so many references to blue herons in my life and never had seen statues of them for sale. Since the appearance of this bird was one of the first messages that Aaron sent, I wanted those statues. I thought to myself "It's crazy what becomes important to you." I purchased the herons and brought them home. Now I could look at them every day and think of Aaron.

I called Melanie and I told her what I had found. She started screaming at the top of her lungs and threw down the phone saying "Hang on. I'll be right back". She was screaming with excitement. She came back to the phone after a minute or two. "Do you remember when I called you and said that Aaron had told me about something that would happen and I wrote it down for you?" I did remember that she had told me that, but I had forgotten about it until now. "Well," she said. "I wrote on this paper that Gayle will tell me something about a blue jay or big blue bird." It's so amazing.

The spirits tell Melanie that there is no time where they are. As humans we cannot seem to grasp this concept. I can't figure out how to work that knowledge into day-to-day experiences. Just how long before hand or how far back, I wonder, are thoughts or situations put into motion, to play out as they do. All I do know for certain is that they are around us even when we think that they are not. Otherwise, how would they know all that was going to happen? It's very comforting for me to know that even when I am not aware of it, my son is still there.

 Melanie was at the same store where she was when her planner was stolen. As she was waiting for her fish fry, Aaron spoke to her. He told her that so much had come from the events of that night. Trust what comes. This was meant to be and it was part of a greater picture. As hard as it is to hear those words, I know that there has to be truth to them. Why else would all this be happening?

 Melanie was coming to my house to pick me up. It was the first time that she had driven here on this route during the daytime. She said that Aaron was with her all the way and that he was so excited that she was going to our house. He was telling her where to go.

As Melanie approached the town of Elbridge, Aaron made her turn her head very abruptly to see something on her right. He was very proud of what he was showing her. Even though she was driving, she looked for what he was trying to show her. She saw the drugstore, but couldn't imagine why he wanted her to look at that. She was trying to look around, but knew that she had passed the spot that he wanted her to see. She was not convinced that the drugstore was what he wanted her to see. When she arrived at our house, she told me what had happened. She asked me if Aaron had worked at that store or if it had some special significance. Unknown to Melanie, the Elbridge Fire Department was right next door to the drugstore. Aaron was a volunteer fireman there and it was one of his passions.

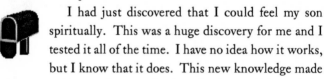 I had just discovered that I could feel my son spiritually. This was a huge discovery for me and I tested it all of the time. I have no idea how it works, but I know that it does. This new knowledge made me so very happy. I got up in the morning and was watching the TV while I had my coffee. The first commercial that played was for the drink Sunny Delight and it said to let your child's spirit shine. Really? Is this a coincidence? I don't think so.

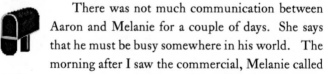 There was not much communication between Aaron and Melanie for a couple of days. She says that he must be busy somewhere in his world. The morning after I saw the commercial, Melanie called me at 7:00am. "Aaron says good morning, Mom!" That night she called again to say that he wanted me to know that they were doing something to honor him at the fire department. Later that week we received an invitation to the annual dinner for the firemen and their families. This was Aaron's fire department, so they invited Tom and me to attend. At the dinner they presented a slide show dedicated to Aaron with wonderful pictures of him. We had no idea that they were honoring Aaron at this dinner. I didn't even make the connection until months later, as I was looking at the sticky note

where I had written down the message. He was trying to prepare us for this upcoming event, even from the other side.

Melanie called tonight and said that Aaron said something to her about peanut butter. She wanted to know if we were eating peanut butter. I told her no. The next morning when Jeffrey got up, out of the blue he said, "I need peanut butter, I need to keep eating a lot of peanut butter for the protein." He took the jar with him to school.

Melanie called in the afternoon and said that Aaron was showing her something with a wooden handle. I didn't have any idea what he was referring to so I thought I should call Tom at work and ask him. I asked him what he was doing before I told him about the phone call. Tom said that he was making a wooden handle for a broom that had broken. No need to say more.

I was folding laundry and Melanie called. "Aaron says to say "plaid" to you". I was folding a plaid flannel shirt. Another time Melanie called when I was folding laundry and he told her to say "plaid boxers". Again, that is exactly what I was folding.

Melanie was driving to her office on Monday night. Aaron was riding with her. He told her that he was excited that his mother could feel him and know that he was there. He said that he didn't want me to hurt anymore.

Aaron tells Melanie that he is with Kyle in the hot tub. He also says that he is being very particular about the holes in the deck- four inches. Kyle was helping his dad build a new deck on the back of our house. Kyle said that he was nailing the decking every four inches.

Aaron was with Melanie as she drove to work again on Monday evening. This is when he usually talks to her the most. He tells her that he has been busy doing other things that is why he hasn't been around. He said that he helps the younger ones as they transition. He also told Melanie that I thought that I felt my grandmother. I had not mentioned this to her, but he confirmed that I did feel her. Amazing! He also said that he was watching the dog tear something up, and that he sent that dog to us. Our dog, Drake, had just torn up a pair of slippers. (The summer after Aaron's death, Kyle, Thomas and Jeffrey found a beautiful puppy at the animal rescue hospital. They brought the dog home for their dad and me. Jeffrey named him Drake.) Aaron also told Melanie that he was calling our phone number. My phone kept on ringing that day, and no one would be there.

Melanie called to say that she was worried about Junior. He is the little brother of Aaron's girlfriend. That day I talked to Malinda and she said that Junior was sick with a fever of 103 degrees.

Toothpicks! We had gone to Baltimore, Maryland for Thomas's lacrosse game. Kyle was living in Arlington, Virginia, so we stayed at a hotel close to him. The night before the game, Kyle, Tom and I went out for dinner. At the restaurant we ordered an appetizer before our dinner and they were called "toothpicks". These toothpicks were very different but also very good. We had dinner, reminisced and talked about Aaron. It was a great evening and it was wonderful to spend time with Kyle. We dropped Kyle off at his apartment and went back to our hotel. Just as we were walking into our room, my cell phone rang. It was Melanie. "Aaron said to say "toothpicks' to you. He is being very specific, not toothpick, but toothpicks with an s".

I love that he is with us wherever we go.

Tom and I were replacing our kitchen floor. After twenty six years and many, many miles, it was time to do so. Melanie called to say that Aaron told her "1/16th". I turned to Tom and he said that he was just saying exactly that to himself; that he was off 1/16th of an inch.

We were all sitting around the table talking after dinner. Kyle was working with his dad at the time, and they were discussing that. Melanie called and said that Aaron told her that they were talking about work and that Kyle had something blue on. He was wearing a blue shirt. Aaron wanted us to know that he was there with us at the table.

It is winter, with lots of snow on the ground. I prayed and prayed for Aaron to send me a sign from him. Even though I receive many messages, I still feel so broken-hearted when I don't hear from him in a while. I look every day for a blue heron to be in our back yard, even though it is rare that one appears. I look for one, though, all of the time. As I am looking out the window, it is snowing and is very grey. Just then a large blue heron flew right in front of me and landed in our yard. That's my boy!

I saw a beautiful red cardinal bird by the side of the road. When I saw it, I immediately thought of Melanie's father-in-law, Pop, and I got chills all over my body, from head to toe. Melanie's father-in-law sends the red Cardinal bird to her as a sign from him that he is close by. I later told Melanie what had happened. She reported that Pop had told her that I would call her with this message for her.

Aaron told Melanie, "Fog Horn, Leg Horn". They are the big cartoon rooster and his little rooster friend. Aaron had the collector glasses of these characters in his room and I was looking at them today. He also said that the blue heron I had seen at the park the previous day was for me.

 I was lying awake in bed; it was late and I could not sleep. Suddenly I could detect the smell of my paternal grandmother's house. It had a very distinct wonderful odor that I recognized immediately. The sensation was brief, but so strong. As soon as I identified what the odor was, I detected just as strongly and just as clearly another fragrance. It was the perfume that my maternal grandmother wore her entire life. Everything that she owned carried the scent of this perfume. There was no doubt either, that I smelled the two aromas. Wow! That was incredible and so comforting.

 Melanie was driving home from work. She hadn't heard from Aaron in a while. Suddenly he pushed very forcibly on her brakes. Just as he did so, a car pulled out in front of her path. He definitely had prevented her from having an accident.

 One of Aaron's favorite things to do was to have a bonfire at our house. The second summer after Aaron's death, Thomas asked one night if he could have friends over for a bonfire too. Melanie called my house as he was standing around the fire with his friends. "Is Thomas by a fire? Aaron says that he is standing by the fire with Thomas", was the message.

 Melanie had a dream of Aaron. In the dream he was wearing camouflage clothing and he was in the woods. He was kneeling down and looked like he had a rifle in his hands. Melanie asked him if he was hunting and he told her that he doesn't hunt where he is, he runs with the deer now.

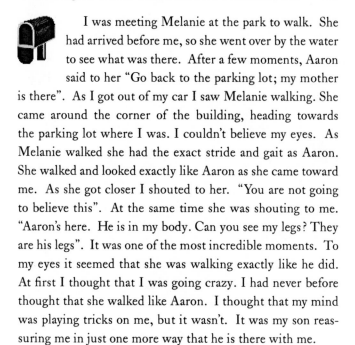

I was meeting Melanie at the park to walk. She had arrived before me, so she went over by the water to see what was there. After a few moments, Aaron said to her "Go back to the parking lot; my mother is there". As I got out of my car I saw Melanie walking. She came around the corner of the building, heading towards the parking lot where I was. I couldn't believe my eyes. As Melanie walked she had the exact stride and gait as Aaron. She walked and looked exactly like Aaron as she came toward me. As she got closer I shouted to her. "You are not going to believe this". At the same time she was shouting to me. "Aaron's here. He is in my body. Can you see my legs? They are his legs". It was one of the most incredible moments. To my eyes it seemed that she was walking exactly like he did. At first I thought that I was going crazy. I had never before thought that she walked like Aaron. I thought that my mind was playing tricks on me, but it wasn't. It was my son reassuring me in just one more way that he is there with me.

Melanie had held one of her group open readings. These events are always so amazing and very uplifting to everyone there. At these events Melanie does random readings as she is pulled to different people all over the room. As you sit with this group of people that you don't even know, you benefit from the messages that everyone is receiving. On the way home from the event I was driving the car and was just about to enter the on ramp to the highway. My mother was in the back seat and my friend Linda was in the front passenger seat. We were talking about all of the wonderful miracles that had been happening and how special the night had been. As we talked, my mother said "I pray and pray and I ask all the time, but I don't get anything from any of our spirits. I don't get any signs or messages." Just then, for reasons unknown to me at that moment, I remembered that I had forgotten to turn my phone back on after the event. So I grabbed my phone and turned it on. As I did, it immediately rang. It was Melanie. All she said was "Aaron says that your mother does too get things; she just doesn't notice." Well, my Mom was pretty quiet for the rest of the ride home.

Melanie was in her kitchen when she felt her father-in-law; Pop. It is not often that his spirit visits her, so when he does she is overjoyed. Melanie was able to have a conversation with him this time. It was almost as though he was standing right there with her. He told her that he takes long walks. That was always one of his favorite things to do. She asked who walked with him. He told her that it was family, some people she knew and some she didn't and that he walks with angels too. He also told her that he was with Aaron and that "He is great". When Melanie later told me about Pop's visit we both said to each other that we were so happy that Aaron was good. Pop shot right back with, "No, he's great!"

We were going to our sister and brother-in-law's home for our family Christmas get-together. A day or so before we were to go, Melanie called and said that Aaron told her to say "Fondue". Well, that didn't have any meaning to me at the time, but I knew enough about how all of this now works. I just needed to be patient and soon enough there would be a connection to fondue. As I was getting things together the evening of the family get-together my sister-in-law called to ask me if I had an extra fondue pot; she was making fondue for the party.

The following miracle was just as meaningful to me as the miracle that first Christmas with Aaron's angel. It's astonishing enough to know and receive messages from our loved ones in spirit, and when they start ganging up together, however, that's really something.

Melanie was moving to a new office and was in the process of decorating it. I very much wanted to get something for Melanie to celebrate her move. She had mentioned that a while ago she had seen a picture of a cardinal and that she loved because it reminded her so much of her beloved father-in-law; Pop. Perfect! I would surprise her with the gift of this cardinal for her office.

When I went to the shop to purchase the artwork, I really wasn't quite sure why she was so attracted to this piece. I knew, though, that she really liked it, so that's what I would get for her. The sales clerk took the piece off the wall, wrapped it, and put it into a box.

On the day that the office decorating was completed, I told her that I had a surprise for her. "Well, no, you don't." She said. "They blew you in and told me and I know what's in the bag." Are you kidding me? Pop and Aaron had told Melanie before I got there what I had for her.

So, as we sat in her office and she took the wrapping off the cardinal, we began to talk about how fortunate we were for all the miracles. Melanie said that Pop used to call her each morning and that more than anything she missed his morning call. As she was telling me this, I looked at the back of the cardinal picture. Neither one of us had looked at the back of it; the salesperson had simply taken it from the wall and wrapped it. As I glanced at it I noticed that written very clearly was the title of this piece: "Morning Call".

 At 5:55a.m. Aaron woke Melanie. She had seen him in her dream. He was smiling and said that he was so happy and wearing his Carhart work overalls. He said to tell me "Happy Mother's Day". She saw him try to call me and saw him push 0 0 0 * 3 on her phone.

She heard those five digits whispered, then the connection was lost. He showed her an angel book that she owns which describes the meaning of numbers. The number 3 and the zeroes indicate that you are doing what you are meant to do, that things have come full circle. Hmmmmm.

 Melanie is shopping in the book store. Aaron tells her to buy the book Saved by the Light, that this book will help me. She calls me from the store to say that she feels so silly talking to me in the middle of the store like this, but he is leading her right to the book and says that she should get it for me. Then he leads her straight to the other side of the store and points out a book that he wants her to read. How weird is this: she is buying the books that my son's spirit is telling her to buy. Well, as you might have noticed by now, there is no arguing with Aaron about anything. Melanie really did not want to get the second book for herself, but he was insistent, so she bought both books. The book that he wanted her to read touched her on so many levels and at times was difficult to read. As she was reading the story, however, she learned of another reason why Aaron wanted her to buy and read this particular book. The story starts out with a man talking about his daughter. He does not mention any other family members in the first part of the book. Then the man's son is introduced into the story. The son is described as a big guy- six foot, three inches tall- and his name is Aaron. The son bounces into the room and says "Hi, Pops!" Is this a coincidence? No, that would be impossible.

 With coaching and encouragement from Aaron, I decided-or should I say that he decided that I would learn Reiki. Reiki is a healing practice that uses energy in the universe.

Would I have been very skeptical of the true legitimacy of this practice before my life had been changed so drastically?

Yes, most likely. Now I know that there is so very, very much that I am unaware of and that Reiki is just one more part of this concept that anything is possible and probable. I know now that there is limitless energy in the universe. I could feel it in Aaron. With his encouragement I really wanted to learn about this practice.

My husband Tom had been suffering from cluster headaches, which come on very quickly with no real remedy or known cause. I met a woman at one of Melanie's events who is a Reiki therapist. I asked her if she could do Reiki for Tom and whether it would help his headaches. She told me that it would help, but, she offered to teach me the technique rather than treat him herself. Wow! I didn't even really know what Reiki was at that time. I couldn't imagine that I could learn such a thing.

You obviously know who was right there with me, so I immediately made an appointment to start the learning process. I would need to go for a Reiki treatment myself prior to learning it, so off I went with no prior knowledge or preconception about Reiki. Suzanne the Reiki Master was administering the Reiki treatment, which is the flow of energy from the universe through her to you. She doesn't even have to touch your body for it to be effective, but I must say that, at the very least, it is one of the most relaxing sensations that you will ever experience. Reiki heals where you need healing. This treatment unblocks your own flow of energy within you, so that your body performs as it was intended to do so. Suzanne did not know much about me, other than the fact that I had lost my son Aaron recently. As I was receiving the treatment, I said "Oh my God, I feel Aaron". Suzanne said, "I know. He is right over there on the couch. I can see him". Wooooh. We were both quite taken by surprise.

This facet of Reiki was just developing for Suzanne and I certainly had no idea that the practice of Reiki could also heighten your intuitive abilities. At first I thought that Suzanne was just another person with intuitive awareness like Melanie's. It never dawned on me that it would also heighten my own awareness.

The next day I was to return for my first Reiki lesson. Melanie had also decided to learn Reiki, so she came along too. The lesson was progressing and we were practicing Reiki treatments as Suzanne showed us the proper hand positions. At exactly the same moment, Melanie and I both said "Aaron's here" and Suzanne said "He's in the same spot on the couch again, watching us."

 I was upstairs late one night thinking of Aaron and talking to him. At 10:00 p.m. I decided to go downstairs. As soon as I walked into the kitchen where I keep my cell phone charging, I heard the signal of a text message coming to my phone. The text was from Melanie and it said "Aaron says that he will always love you." I could not believe that she sent that message at that moment. He really does hear my words. I texted back to her how amazing he is. Melanie texted me again and asked if Tom was eating ice cream then? No, but Jeffrey was. I decided that maybe I should bring my phone upstairs with me, which is something that I rarely do.

As I was heading back up the stairs with my phone, another text arrived from Melanie: "Maybe you should bring your phone to bed." I should have known that there was more to come. I returned to bed and continued reading, for the second time, the book Saved by the Light. This is the book that Aaron told Melanie that I should read. I was reading the part that describes when the man in the book dies, is lifted to heaven, and sees the Being of light. It doesn't mention anyone else being there with him and I was wondering if this was what Aaron's experience was like. Was he confused; was he scared; was he all alone? At that very moment I received a text. In the text Melanie said that she had been sleeping and that Aaron woke her up and said "I am with God." He told her to relay this message to me. She also said that there was a woman with Aaron and that her name was Mary. My grandmother who has passed was named Mary.

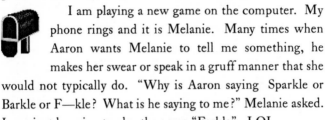 I am playing a new game on the computer. My phone rings and it is Melanie. Many times when Aaron wants Melanie to tell me something, he makes her swear or speak in a gruff manner that she would not typically do. "Why is Aaron saying Sparkle or Barkle or F—kle? What is he saying to me?" Melanie asked. I was just learning to play the game "Farkle". LOL

It's my birthday today. What I want above all else is for Aaron to come back home to me. I keep thinking to myself that if only he could come home and give me a hug. I would hug him, too. I keep going over in my mind the list of people who are dear to me who have passed. I ask them all to give Aaron a hug from me right now. A close friend of ours has also passed away recently, so in my mind I ask Aaron to help him with his transition, and to give him a hug from us too.

Later that afternoon, Melanie calls me on her way home from work. "Hey, it's your boy!" she says. "I was wondering where he's been all day, saying to him: Come on, Aaron, it's your Mom's birthday today. Aren't you going to show up on her birthday? And here he is! He says to say "Bear Hug" to you". He never, ever lets me down.

Shortly after I started working for Melanie and was introduced to this world of spirit existence, I decided that I would try, with all of my being, to open up my channels of communication. Perhaps I would be able to contact Aaron. I was completely new to this way of thinking, but I was determined to work at it. I did not tell anyone, however, that this was what I was trying to do. I thought that if Melanie could do it, then maybe I could too-even if only a little. I listened to guided meditation tapes, read everything that I could find and researched any information that might be available. I had merely uncovered the tip of the iceberg, but each discovery led me to something new.

One day I was listening to a guided meditation lesson that I had. I was working hard at understanding the techniques of meditation. I was listening to the lesson that explained what a spirit guide is and how to discover your own spirit guide. What's a spirit guide I wondered? I wondered whether it is someone else who has these abilities to communicate with the dead.

As I listened to the guided meditation lesson, I did what the instructor told me to do. He said to close my eyes while concentrating on my breathing. After several minutes he instructed me with his voice to visualize walking into a field where I would come upon a house. I was to walk up to this house, knock on the door, and my spirit guide would answer the door. The instructor said that I could talk to my spirit guide and ask a question; there may be more than one spirit guide.

As I listened to the instructions these images actually did appear in my mind. I did see myself walking into a field and there was a house. I knocked on the door and it was answered by a big, burly man, complete with kilt, matted hair and scruffy red beard. He looked like the character from the movie; "Braveheart". I know that in my mind this person spoke his name to me, but I cannot remember the name that he gave. However, after meeting this spirit guide in the kilt, I turned to my right and there was another door. When this second door opened, I clearly saw in my mind a very tall, slender man who was dressed in a 1950's style black suit. He had on a very thin black tie, white shirt and a hat from that time period. He said that his name was Cliff. I remember his name very vividly, even though I cannot remember the name of the first man.

Well, I thought this all very strange and really didn't think that this meditation/ spirit guide experience had really worked. I thought that I was making up the story as I listened along with the instructor. I wasn't really sure what a spirit guide does, so how would I know if I had actually met one? Time went on and I did not talk about this particular lesson to very many people, but I did say to a friend that I remembered the man named Cliff. I simply thought that it was an interesting lesson and I wanted to keep learning about the spirit world.

Almost two years after this experience my friend Melanie was at our house and she said to me: "Dennis and Cliff came to me last night. Cliff says to tell you that he is with you, that he is always by your side helping you." My mouth actually fell open in amazement. I hadn't mentioned anything about that Meditation lesson to Melanie. I couldn't believe it. I am not so sure that Dennis is the name of the first spirit guide whom I met. The name does seem very familiar, however, for some reason. I do know for certain that the name of the second spirit guide that day two years ago was definitely Cliff.

This happened at the very beginning of my quest. Somehow that day my spirit guide did get through to me; I just didn't know it. I have learned more about spirit guides as each day goes by. They are ever present by your side; should you ever need them. You only have to ask and they are willing to assist you in any way that they can. We all have lessons to learn while on this earth; our spirit guides are willing and able to help us along the way. We each have our own; specific spirit guide or guides; that are there to help us alone.

Aaron College 2007   *Aaron's Angel*

Family Picture

Dads plaque that he made for Aaron

Gayle & Melanie

Gayle Thanksgiving with an orb on right shoulder

Tom on Thanksgilving Day 2008 with orb above his head

Jeffrey 2008 hunting his first turkey

Kyle & Thomas 2008 National Lacrosse Championship

Winter 2008 Blue Heron
in our pond

PART III

Chapter Sixteen

Do You Believe?

So now you know all about, our tragic, unexpected; breathtaking journey since the accident that took my son Aaron's life on that night in May of 2008.

Some people would say that I have gone crazy, that I lost my senses trying to deal with such a loss. Many days I think that to lose my mind would be a blessing as long as the pain in my heart would be gone too. You might say that I was grasping at anything in order to hear what I wanted so desperately to hear.

I have accused myself of that very thing many times, only to receive another miracle and confirmation. They shout at me to listen with my heart as well as with my head, and prove to me undoubtedly that my son is still here. What matters to me the most is that Aaron is okay, happy and well without me. He reassures me again and again that he is doing just fine. I am the one who is missing him so.

I know that what I have experienced is true and real, although many times it seems like it is coincidence or staged. However, it is not.

I know that these miracles do not happen to me alone. I answer the calls that come into Melanie's office from strangers all over the country. I know that each caller needs the healing gift that Melanie has more than I need it at that moment. Some callers are apprehensive and nervous; many want to share with me their amazing stories of miracles that have happened to them. Each story that I hear reinforces my belief that this connection is real and lifts my heart.

I know that gaining the knowledge that I now have was at the insistence of my son. The knowledge of interactive existence between our loved ones' spirits and us can help to heal so many broken hearts. As Melanie always says, "It all comes from Love".

CHAPTER SEVENTEEN

The Mailbox

Shortly after Aaron's death, my brother David had placed a mailbox at Aarons' grave. He had also done this for his daughter Jennifer, when she passed away from cancer at the age of fifteen. The mailbox was for anyone who wished to write a message, letter, poem, or whatever they felt, to Aaron. Although I was so grateful to David for thinking of this and I was sure that it is very healing to many of Aaron's visitors, I could not bring myself to put anything in the mailbox or look to see who may have. What was the point? He was gone: he couldn't read it; and I just wanted him back.

Well, as you may have figured out by now; Aaron can be very persistent. I now realize that Aaron wasn't going to let his meaning for the mailbox go unnoticed. I am quite sure that he is responsible for the mailbox; even though my brother may have thought it his idea alone. I now understand that the mailbox is where we can place our written messages to Aaron but he reads them anyway; even if we don't put them in the box. He hears us whenever we talk to him whether we speak the words out- loud or only in our minds. He constantly sends messages to us too. Are you listening? Are you watching? Aaron's Mailbox is available to us all; receiving and sending messages so that we know that he loves us.

So where do I go with all of this newfound enlightenment? Are we all meant to know now without a doubt that all of our loved ones who have passed on are but a thought away? Isn't this the same message that has been circulated throughout the years? It was presented to me in dramatic fashion. Perhaps that was the best way to get my attention. I have learned for certain that the message that our loved ones have for us, the only message that really matters is that they love us. Their methods of delivering this message may be diverse. Sometimes they may be difficult to hear. Ultimately, however, it's always the same: they love us.

I love you Aaron.

CPSIA information can be obtained at www.ICGtesting.com
Printed in the USA
BVOW03s1104310713

327412BV00001B/1/P